THE COLLECTED POETRY OF CAROL SHIELDS

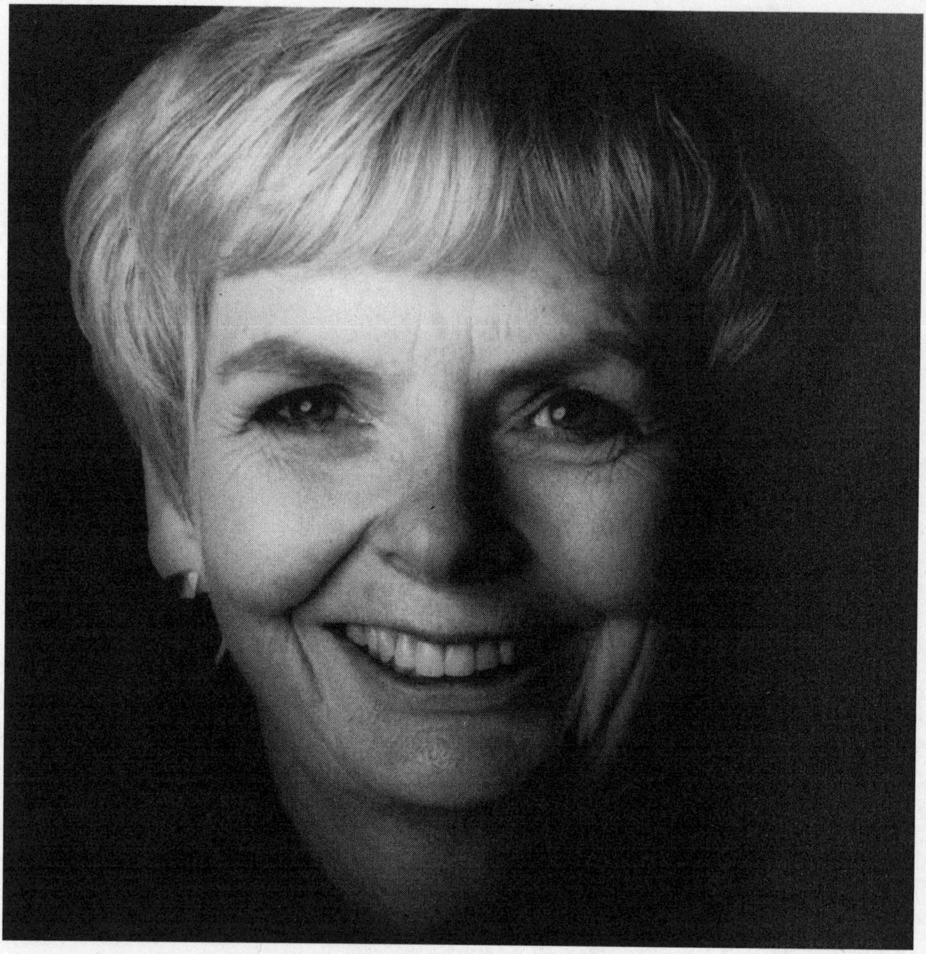

THE COLLECTED POETRY OF

Carol Shields

EDITED BY NORA FOSTER STOVEL

MCGILL-QUEEN'S UNIVERSITY PRESS
Montreal & Kingston • London • Chicago

© Estate of Carol Shields 2021
Introduction and critical apparatus © McGill-Queen's University Press 2021

ISBN 978-0-2280-0886-6 (cloth)
ISBN 978-0-2280-0887-3 (paper)
ISBN 978-0-2280-1022-7 (ePDF)
ISBN 978-0-2280-1023-4 (ePUB)

Legal deposit fourth quarter 2021
Bibliothèque nationale du Québec

Printed in Canada on acid-free paper that is 100% ancient forest free (100% post-consumer recycled), processed chlorine free

This book has been published with the help of a grant from the Carol Shields Literary Trust.

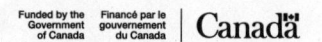

We acknowledge the support of the Canada Council for the Arts.
Nous remercions le Conseil des arts du Canada de son soutien.

LIBRARY AND ARCHIVES CANADA CATALOGUING IN PUBLICATION

Title: The collected poetry of Carol Shields / edited by Nora Foster Stovel.
Other titles: Poems
Names: Shields, Carol, author. | Stovel, Nora Foster, 1942– editor.
Description: Includes bibliographical references.
Identifiers: Canadiana (print) 20210236817 | Canadiana (ebook) 2021023685X |
    ISBN 9780228008866 (hardcover) | ISBN 9780228008873 (softcover) |
    ISBN 9780228010227 (PDF) | ISBN 9780228010234 (ePUB)
Subjects: LCSH: Shields, Carol—Criticism and interpretation. | CSH: Canadian poetry (English)—20th century—History and criticism. | LCGFT: Poetry.
Classification: LCC PS8587 .H46 2021 | DDC C811/.54—dc23

FOR CAROL SHIELDS AND THE SHIELDS FAMILY

CONTENTS

- xv   Books by Carol Shields
- xvii   Foreword | After Enlightenment: The Poetry of Carol Shields
  Jan Zwicky
- xxiii   Acknowledgments
- xxv   A Note on the Text with Abbreviations
- xxvii   Introduction | The Collected Poetry of Carol Shields
  Nora Foster Stovel

POEMS BY CAROL SHIELDS

- 2   **Others**
- 4   A Woman We Know Who Suffers from Occasional Depression
- 5   Advice from a Green-Thumbed Friend
- 6   Margaret at Easter
- 7   The Ferryman at Prince Edward County
- 9   Some Old Friends Who Flew to England
- 10   The New Mothers
- 12   A Woman We Saw in an Antique Shop
- 13   A Cynical Friend Explains
- 14   Anne at the Symphony
- 15   A Fiftyish Aunt
- 16   Grandpa Who Is Eighty at the Cottage
- 17   A Husband Thinks Out Loud
- 18   Insomniac
- 19   Sara
- 20   A Member of the Bridge Club
- 21   Michael, A Boy in Our Neighbourhood

22	A Married Couple
23	Child Who Is Falling Asleep
24	An Old Lady We Saw
25	Our Artist Friends
27	Our Old Aunt Who Is Now in a Retirement Home
28	A Professor We Know Who Is a Compulsive Storyteller
29	Someone I Don't Like Anymore and Never Really Did
30	No One's Simple, Not Even Sally
31	Someone We Met Who Grew Up on a Farm
32	Our Old Professor
33	Someone Hurrying Home
34	Someone We've Heard a Lot About
35	The Stocking Man
36	John
37	Helen's Morning
38	A Family Cycling By
39	Great-Grandma
40	Two Old Friends Who Arrived at Dawn
41	A Wife, Forty-Five, Remembers Love
42	Grandma's Things
44	What Our Toronto Friends Said
46	An Old Couple Who Have Loved Each Other
47	A Friend of Ours Who Knits
49	A Physicist We Know
50	Someone We Haven't Seen in Years
52	Two Little Girls Dressed as Witches
53	An East Coast Friend of Ours Writes from the West
55	A Wedding We Went to Once
57	An Acquaintance of Ours Who Is an Obsessive Christian
58	The Barman in Halifax
59	The Dean's Wife
60	A Friend About to Be Divorced
61	A Mother We Know Who Has Many Children
62	A Member of Parliament

63 Intersect

64 Pioneers: Southeast Ontario
65 Mother
66 Friend: After Surgery
67 Aunt Alice Recalled
68 Reading in Bed
69 Woman at a Party
70 Professor
71 Suppertime 1950
72 Margaret, Aged Four
73 Service Call
74 Emily Dickinson
75 Rough Riders
77 Accidents
78 Volkswagen
79 Sister
80 After the Party: I
81 After the Party: II
82 Radio Announcer
83 Child Learning to Talk
84 A Couple Take a Sunday Drive
86 Letter from a Friend
87 William
88 Betty
89 Fetus
90 Our Mother's Friends
92 Class in Evolution
93 Couple
94 Singer
96 Home Movies 1962
97 Old Friend – Long Distance
98 Uncle
99 Helen Lighting a Fire

100 Old Men
101 Friend of a Friend
102 Picnic at the Lake
103 Daughter
104 A Couple Celebrate Their Silver Anniversary
105 Someone We Saw
106 Family Friend, Aged Ninety
107 An Actor in the Little Theatre
108 Family at the Cottage
109 Poet
110 Sunbathers: Canada
111 January
112 Boys Playing Chess
113 Neighbour
114 Carolers: Ontario
115 Boy Waking Up
116 Circles
117 As for Us

118 Coming to Canada

120 Getting Born
122 Learning to Talk
123 I/Myself
124 Another Birth
125 The Radio –1940
126 Daddy
127 When Grandma Died – 1942
129 The Methodist Jesus
131 The Four Seasons
133 Visiting Aunt Violet
134 Learning to Read
135 Waking and Sleeping
137 Easter

- *138* Aunt Ada
- *139* The End of the War – 1945
- *140* Entry
- *141* Snow
- *142* Being Happy – 1949
- *144* Vision
- *145* Dog Days
- *146* Away from Home – 1954
- *147* Love – Age 20
- *149* Gifts
- *150* Coming to Canada – Age Twenty-Two

151 **"New Poems"** (from *Coming to Canada*)

- *153* Sunday Painter
- *155* Sleeping
- *156* Accident
- *157* Believe Me
- *158* Confession
- *159* Remembering
- *160* Whenever
- *161* Voices
- *162* Journey
- *163* Relics
- *164* Fortune
- *166* Aunt Violet's Things
- *167* The Invention of Clocks
- *168* At the Clock Museum
- *169* Now
- *170* Quartz
- *171* Calendar Notes
- *172* Getting
- *173* Caragana
- *174* Spring

175 Cold Storage
177 Tenth Reunion
178 Daylight Saving
179 House
180 The Class of '53 – Thirty Years Later
182 Wedding
183 Holiday
184 Falling Back
186 Fall
188 Together
189 Work
190 Walkers
191 Season's Greetings

192 Mary Swann's Poems in *Swann*

193 Part One: Sarah Maloney
195 Part Two: Morton Jimroy
196 Part Three: Rose Hindmarch
198 Part Four: Frederick Cruzzi
200 Lost Things

201 *Snow* Poem Sequence (previously unpublished)

232 "Time Line" Poem Sequence (previously unpublished)

233 Others
234 Laughter – Aged 16
235 Sunday Outing
236 All Day Long
237 Snapshot: Your face
238 Blame
239 At the Cottage
241 England

242 Expatriate
243 Somebody
244 Getting to Know
245 Cliché
246 The Fall
247 Likeness
248 Coping
249 Being Sad 1949

250 The Sunday Poems (previously unpublished)

Untitled poems are identified by their first line.
251 "Beside me on the plane"
252 "Some people, doing the cathedrals"
253 Other
255 Shock
256 Inside Sunday

257 Archived Poems (previously unpublished)

258 Learning to Write Poems
259 Going to Work
260 Sonnet
261 Couple
262 The Tea Ceremony
263 Mark Twain
265 Napoleon at St. Helena
267 Letters
268 Holiday
269 April in Ottawa

271 Annotations
279 Works Cited

BOOKS BY CAROL SHIELDS

NOVELS

Small Ceremonies
The Box Garden
Happenstance
A Fairly Conventional Woman
Swann: A Mystery
A Celibate Season (with Blanche Howard)
The Republic of Love
The Stone Diaries
Larry's Party
Unless

SHORT STORIES

Various Miracles
The Orange Fish
Dressing Up for the Carnival
Collected Stories

POETRY

Others
Intersect
Coming to Canada

PLAYS

Departures and Arrivals
Thirteen Hands
Fashion, Power, Guilt and the Charity of Families (with Catherine Shields)
Anniversary: A Comedy (with Dave Williamson)
Women Waiting
Unless
Larry's Party – the Musical
(adapted by Richard Ouzounian with music by Marek Norman)
Thirteen Hands and Other Plays

CRITICISM

Susanna Moodie: Voice and Vision

BIOGRAPHY

Jane Austen: A Life

ANTHOLOGIES

Dropped Threads: What We Aren't Told (edited with Marjorie Anderson)
Dropped Threads 2: More of What We Aren't Told
(edited with Marjorie Anderson)

ESSAYS

Startle and Illuminate: Carol Shields on Writing

FOREWORD

After Enlightenment
The Poetry of Carol Shields

Jan Zwicky

THE 1950S. An extraordinary decade in white middle-class America and its Canadian satellite: the boys home from the wars, the industrial economy booming, colonial culture once again celebrating sharply defined gender roles. Middle-class white women were terrorized by the threat of *what people would think* if they failed to measure up. The rapes in the backseats and married bedrooms went unmentioned, the suicides in the kitchens were erased. The other side of town appeared in peripheral vision only.

This is the culture in which Carol Shields came of age. In her work, the other side of town is rarely brought into focus and the rapes remain unspoken, but there is a growing awareness of female suicidal despair, building rage at the powerlessness of women regardless of the leafiness of their suburbs. The first line of Shields's poem "The End of the War – 1945" is "There was our mother." Exactly. It was an era that idolized the unexamined comfiness of family life. At the heart of this idyll was Betty Crocker: high-heeled, waist cinched to twenty-two inches, in the kitchen. Shields's work does not instruct the white middle class to check its privilege; what it does instead is invite us all to check *behind* that privilege.

The power of Shields's work does not, however, rest exclusively in its perception of the dark underside of middle-class optimism: it resides in the tension between that dark underside and the dream of middle-class happiness: a cherishing of togetherness, of comfort, stability, laughter, and ease. And isn't belief in that dream the reason that those of us who do have privilege must check it? Aren't comfort, ease, stability, and laughter what everyone wants? Respect, too, yes; but respect as the first step toward physical and mental well-being.

What no one wants is the condescension that is often visited on those who actually keep the idyll ticking over – who cook the meals, take care of the sick kids, and clean the toilets. It is a condescension that extends to women who write about domestic concerns. They are described as "discovering the magic of ordinary experiences," praised for the "visionary quality" of their rendering of the "all-too-ordinary."[1] It's that word "ordinary." No one uses it to praise Catullus or Wordsworth or Billy Collins or Philip Larkin. It is a way, even while acknowledging achievement, of saying that the work is not great, that it can never be great. Greatness is for men.

Except it isn't.

A Member of Parliament

Here you can see
politicians viewed from the top,
foreshortened on green carpet,
who wander about, whisper, pop
up and down, shout
and shuffle paper, discuss
with fire or doze
through afternoons of history.

Imagine if you can
one of those
bald heads lifted out
of its walnut horizons
and studied in silhouette.

> Then
> it becomes a mere man,
> someone
> misspelled on a list
> who scarcely matters or even
> exists
>
> like one of us. (62)

An interest in "mere" women and men – our strivings for happiness, their systematic thwarting in the case of many women, their occasional self-sabotage in the case of some men – permeates all of Shields's work. Are these concerns manifest in her poetry in a particular way? Does the *medium* of poetry allow them to manifest in a particular way?

Shields's poems consist overwhelmingly of lyric character studies: dispassionate, penetrating portraits of *others* – people she has encountered only briefly as well as some she knows well. Character, as Aristotle remarked, is essential to dramatic narrative. It is certainly possible to reflect on it independently of narrative, but doing so is unusual. Storytelling is character's natural home. Even the deep, oneirically structured storytelling of myth is concerned with the interaction between character and event.

The lyric aspect of Shields's work, on the other hand, pulls in a different direction. Lyric vision is most frequently concerned with how some individual thing or situation – an old Greek urn, a bee-loud glade, a 1943 valentine fluttering from a book – opens on the atemporal or temporally cyclic vista of being. One of the defining features of lyric utterance is its insight into the fundamental coherence of the world, the interconnectedness of things. Any moment, any hummingbird feather, is capable of revealing the resonance of the whole because every moment is, in fact, informed by the resonance of the whole. Lyric vision does not transform the ordinary; it reveals that "ordinariness" does not exist. And while lyric poetry does not confine itself to the natural world, an interest in the natural world is an easy fit, partly because that world, in and of itself, does not involve plots in the storyteller's sense.

Shields's poetry thus balances itself – remarkably – between one of the classic preoccupations of a novelist and an unswerving allegiance to lyric metaphysics. Even the long sequence "Coming to Canada" does not tell a story. We never, in fact, learn how Shields ended up moving across the border. The twenty-nine poems of the previously unpublished sequence "Snow" are character portraits; the snow serves merely as a backdrop (and perhaps an overarching metaphor for pain) against which the two nineteenth-century sisters and the twentieth-century researcher seek connection with others. The stanzas written in Mary Swann's voice in the novel that bears her name draw their images from the natural world, but only to record its violence, its harshness, its evasiveness, its presence as a setting for the absence of comforting human contact. Shields, in her own voice, says,

Confession

An anxious twitch of the nerves
    is all I get
    from sunsets, meadows, birds
    and all that

Mountains go flat
    on me and trees fall
but time's tenanted chronicle
    fills me full (158)

It is to the gestures, the interior monologues, the unmended socks, and fading snapshots of the individual tenants of history that Shields turns the full power of her lyric gaze.

In its focus on apparently inconsequential detail the power of lyric insight becomes most palpable: this, *even this*, reveals the enormous scope of being. If we see the detail truly – which is what lyric attention positions us to do – we sense the resonance of the entire world through it. Or as Shields puts it, "jars, teaspoons, loaves of bread ... take on the look of sacred objects when seen in exceptional light."[2] There is thus a politics at the heart of lyric utterance, and it is the deep politics of Shields's poetry. If lyric insight is true, then "greatness" is a chimerical construction of human insecurity. Being itself has no centres; it lives in the resonance of every aspect with every other, including the resonance of human individuals with other human individuals. That resonance is the source of human joy, she argues, and separation from it, deafness or blindness to it, is the source of pain and grief. The most powerful lyric poems allow us to feel the extraordinary, unbearable, imminent pressure of enormity in the unregarded, in what *appears* – because we don't attend to it – to be inconsequential. In general, lyric attention gives the lie to the myth of the inconsequential. In particular, Shields's lyric character studies give the lie to the myth of the inconsequential life.

Before enlightenment, chopping carrots and doing laundry.
After enlightenment: chopping carrots and doing laundry.

JAN ZWICKY, Heriot Ridge, British Columbia

NOTES

1 From Eric Thompson's review of Shields's *Intersect* in *Canadian Literature* 65 (Summer 1975): 101–4 at 102, subsequently used on the back cover of the 1997 printing of that book; and from an obituary for Eavan Boland in the *Economist*, 16 May 2020, 82.
2 Carol Shields, *Swann*, 1st ed. (Toronto: Stoddart, 1987; Penguin, 1990), 208.

ACKNOWLEDGMENTS

I WISH TO ACKNOWLEDGE, first and foremost, Carol Shields's family, especially Don Shields, as well as Karen McDiarmaid and the Carol Shields Literary Estate. I also wish to thank the Social Sciences and Humanities Council of Canada for the Strategic Grant that enabled me to research the Shields Archives at the National Library, and the University of Alberta Faculty of Arts for the McCalla professorships that allowed me to edit this collection of Shields's complete poetry. I am grateful to the previous editors Christopher Levenson and John Flood for their cooperation, and to Philip Cercone, Kathleen Fraser, and the friendly staff of McGill-Queen's University Press. I am also grateful to the two excellent readers who contributed such helpful suggestions; to my copy editor, Kate Merriman, once again, for her meticulous work; and to my editors Mark Abley and Philip Cercone for their valuable advice and guidance. Joanne Pisano, Madison Karcs, and Marcie Whitecotton-Carroll provided expert technical assistance, and Cathie Crooks, Peter Midgley, Ruth Panofsky, Bella Pomer, and Mindy Werner provided invaluable encouragement and support of this project.

A Note on the Text

ALL PREVIOUSLY PUBLISHED POEMS, including fifty from *Others* (1972), fifty from *Intersect* (1974), and seventy-nine from *Coming to Canada* (1992), have been reproduced exactly as published. In the rare instances where a typographical or other error has occurred, they have been corrected silently. Previously unpublished poems have been reproduced as they appear in Shields's archives in the National Library. Differences between versions of poems published and archived, as well as Shields's emendations in archived poems, have been annotated.

The following abbreviations are employed:

BG	*The Box Garden*
CC	*Coming to Canada*
CP	*Collected Poetry*
CS	*A Celibate Season*
EV	*Early Voices*
H	*Happenstance*
I	*Intersect*
LP	*Larry's Party*

MF	*A Memoir of Friendship*
NH	*Narrative Hunger"*
O	*Others*
R	*The Republic of Love*
RI	*Random Illuminations*
SC	*Small Ceremonies*
SD	*The Stone Diaries*
SI	*Startle and Illuminate: Carol Shields on Writing*
U	*Unless*

INTRODUCTION

The Collected Poetry of Carol Shields

Nora Foster Stovel

Poetry was the prism that refracted all of life. It was Jimroy's belief that the best and worst of human experiences were frozen inside these wondrous little toys called poems.

Swann (86)

CAROL SHIELDS is most famous for her fiction, but few admirers of her novels are aware that her first published books were collections of poetry. In fact, she published over 160 poems in three collections – *Others* in 1972, *Intersect* in 1974, and *Coming to Canada* in 1992 – the first two before she ever published a novel.[1] As Christopher Levenson observes in his introduction to *Coming to Canada*, "few people are familiar with the poetry that made up her first two publications, and many are even now unaware that she writes poetry" (xi). Calgary poet Christopher Wiseman calls Shields a *wordsmith*: "It should surprise nobody who is familiar with her deft, precise, witty, fluent, subtle use of language that she is also a poet" (65). Levenson aims to illuminate "this too little-known aspect of Carol Shields' many-sided talent" (xxv) because "an acquaintance with the poetry can illuminate or focus aspects of the novels" (xi). I hope to extend that illumination through this new edition of her collected poetry, including both previously published and previously unpublished poems, through analysis of the poetry itself and through relating her poetry to her fiction, contextualizing it in her oeuvre.

Poetry, I suggest, is the secret to Shields's success as a writer: besides the excellence of her poetry itself, her poetry influenced and informed her fiction, not only by encouraging her to discover *le mot juste* but because she employed metaphors in her fiction that she first developed in her poetry to convey the epiphanic moment. Her development as a poet, beginning with her juvenilia, is fascinating.

Shields started writing poetry – mainly metrical, rhymed poems – as a schoolgirl in Oak Park, Illinois, which her former creative writing student, author Martin Levin, labels a "churchgoing Norman Rockwell town" (14), a town that produced three Pulitzer prizewinners: novelist Ernest Hemingway, poet Charles Simic, and writer Carol Shields, who beat out the other finalists of that year, Joyce Carol Oates and Grace Paley. She told Eleanor Wachtel that she kept thinking that they would call to say they'd made a mistake and intended to award the prize to Joyce Carol Oates (Levin 15).

Shields recalls writing "Little ditties. Class plays" (Wachtel, 1989, 12). She records, "I wrote as a child. I was a schoolgirl writer. Every school has one of these girls, you know, who writes the class play, and writes the class poem, and everyone says, 'Oh, you're going to be a writer when you grow up.' I didn't, in fact, think I would. It felt like wanting to be a movie star."[2] She considered writers "exotic creatures," although she had never met any (*RI* 116). She recalls, "I very early formed the notion of being a writer, all the while knowing that this was impossible. Writers were like movie stars. Writers were men" (York 145). After attending Nathaniel Hawthorne School (now named Percy Julian Middle School after the African-American chemist) and Ralph Waldo Emerson School (now named Gwendolyn Brooks Middle School after the African-American poet), she reflected, "They were writers, they were men, they were dead"

(Levin 14). She had "an inspiring teacher who treated us as if we were going to be writers" (Levin 14), however, and recalls "discovering poetry and all the things that were important to me as a child" (*RI* 79).

Her earliest ambition was to be a poet: "I used to say I was going to be a poet when I grew up. I had no idea what that meant. But I was lavishly praised for the execrable poetry I wrote – I can't tell you how bad it was." Ever modest, she adds, "Sometimes I think that's why I became a writer, because I really couldn't do anything else very well" (*RI* 31).

She particularly enjoyed writing sonnets as a girl: "I always carried around in my bag the sonnet I was working on at that particular moment" (*RI* 116). She recalls, "I was the class poet and right through high school I loved to write sonnets. They were an attempt to use the sort of language I now despise in poetry – for example, pretty language." She explains that, later, "I followed Larkin's set of rules. No pretty language. If anything was pretty, out it went" (Wachtel, 1989, 22). She adds, "Unfortunately I also borrowed some of his despair, I think, in my first few poems" (Wachtel, 1989, 22). Her friends feared she was contemplating suicide.

In *Larry's Party* (1997) Shields's narrator recalls "the time of the old poetry, 1977, when the world rhymed and chimed" (298), but 1957 might be more accurate, since the style of poetry that Shields subscribed to as a budding writer was popular then. She referred to the "exceedingly WASP suburb of Chicago" in which she grew up as "a plastic bag" (Thomas 122), suggesting a secure, conventional environment. Some female critics have considered her poetry too restrained, too *nice*, because, as Wiseman affirms, "her poetry does not raise its voice or stamp its feet, does not rage or slash at life" (69), but it is essential to contextualize Shields's early verse in her era, class, and gender. In the fifties, the old adage, "If you can't say something nice, don't say anything at all" applied particularly to young women. In fact, in a preamble to her essay "Arriving Late: Starting Over," Shields affirms, "I was brought up believing it was impolite to talk about one's self – impolite for everyone, and especially for girls" (Carol Shields Fonds, Accession 2003–09, Box 112, File 1).

In her essay "A View from the Edge," Shields records, "I began, quite early, to write: stories, often with a supernatural theme and a trick ending. I also wrote little poems about spring, and later, as I mastered the mechanics of meter, *sonnets* about spring. All of what I wrote was derivative in the extreme and yet all enthusiastically applauded by my teachers and parents. 'Satin-slippered April,' one of these sonnets began, 'You glide through time and lubricate spring days'" (Dvořák 19). She adds parenthetically, "(Spring clearly served as a metaphor of some kind, or else provided a safe cover beneath which I could speak of other less admissible passions)." She includes this line verbatim in *Unless* (2002), as Reta Winters, her narrator, recalls her "old schoolgirl sonnets from the seventies – Satin-slippered April, you glide through time / And lubricate spring days" (2) – revealing connections between Shields's poetry and prose, and suggesting her meta-autobiographical impulse. Shields acknowledges that, "like my mother, who never threw out two tablespoons of leftover peas if she could help it" (*SI* 24), she had a thrifty habit of recycling images and other items, a habit reflected, for example, in her short story "A Scarf," which is included in *Unless*, or her story "By Mistake," which provides the opening section of *Larry's Party*.

Although no sonnets are included in her three previous collections, we do have "Sonnet," published in *Thoughts*, the literary magazine of her alma mater, Hanover College, in 1957. It is a love poem addressed to Donald Hugh Shields, whom she married later that year.[3] After rejecting the approaches to love of Milton, Byron, and Elizabeth Barrett Browning, the poet's persona inquires, "Dare I trust myself?" and concludes with her own definition:

> when they ask me what love is I'll say
> That feeling that you give me when you're near.
> You are my definition. You alone
> Can tell me what the poets have not known.[4] (260)

Shields returned to the sonnet form in her final, unfinished novel, "Moment's Moment," revised by her daughter, poet Sara Cassidy, and published posthumously as "Segue" (1–20), the first entry in *The Collected Stories* (2003).[5] Jane Sexton, the protagonist/narrator, is president of the American Sonnet Society and composes a sonnet each fortnight. This novel was structured in fourteen chapters, reflecting the sonnet form, which Shields visualized as glass shelves. She subscribed to Leonardo da Vinci's maxim: "Art breathes from containment and suffocates from freedom" (*SI* 61). Shields told me in a May 2003 interview that she was currently attempting to compose a sonnet for the novel, which, she lamented, was "in fragments on my Apple."[6] Before her death in July 2003, she told Eleanor Wachtel, "I'd love to write the sonnet novel but I don't seem to have the energy" (*RI* 13).

Poetry actually frames her novels: her first, unpublished novel, *The Vortex*, features poets engaged in producing a poetry magazine, and she was planning to return to poetry in the novel she was composing at the time of her death, as previously mentioned. In *The Vortex*, several poets display an array of different poetic styles, contrasting Victorian modes of versification with more modern, bohemian styles. Its title reflects Ezra Pound's 1914 essay "Vortex" published in Wyndham Lewis's poetry magazine *Blast*. Moreover, two of her published novels, *The Box Garden* (1977) and *Swann* (1987), focus on poets.[7]

Most writers feel shamefaced about their juvenilia, and Shields is no exception. In the author's introduction to her juvenilia in a 2001 anthology entitled *Early Voices*, she confesses, "I suppose that, like all writers, I feel rather sheepish about my early writing" (10). As a mature writer, she came to despise pretty poetry: "Not long ago, I was going through old mementoes and I found one of my poems printed on the graduation program, and it was really embarrassing. Naturally, it was in conventional metre, it rhymed and ended with 'Going toward the future wherein awaits the end of every dream.'" She adds, "And the thing is, I knew then that it wasn't true. I knew that was false rhetoric. But it was part of the rhetoric of the day. For my thirty-fifth high school reunion, I've been asked to write a new poem, and the line I'm starting with is: 'We were all white'" (*RI* 29–30). "The Class of '53 – Thirty Years Later" (180) may be the poem she is referring to here.

At Oak Park and River Forest High School, she wrote poetry in earnest, most of it, she later judged, "amateurish and corny" (*EV* 9). Some poems were odes to autumn or spring and filled with "terrible metaphors" and "outrageous clichés" (*EV* 9). She published poems in *The Crest*, the school's student publication, and later in *Thoughts*, the literary magazine of Hanover College – poems now housed in the National Archives.

Writers learn their craft through imitation, as Margaret Atwood observed in a November 2020 virtual launch of *Early Writings by Margaret Atwood*. Shields's early poems are very well written, although they reflect an earlier period and style. Thus, some are composed in rhyming couplets and reflect the influence of nineteenth-century English poets such as Tennyson and Browning or early twentieth-century American poets such as Carl Sandburg.[8]

In Shields's 1977 novel *The Box Garden*, protagonist-poet Charleen Forrest confesses to imitating others: "My first poems were experiments; I built them on borrowed rhythms; I was a dedicated tinkerer, putting together the shapes and ideas which I shoplifted." She adds, "I found that I could, with a little jiggling, produce images of quite startling vividness. My first poems were lit with a whistling blue clarity (emptiness), and they were accepted by the first magazine I sent them to. Only I knew what paste-up jobs they were, only I silently acknowledged my debt to a good thesaurus, a stimulating dictionary and a daily injection, administered like Vitamin B, of early Eliot. I, who manufactured the giddy, dark-edged metaphors, knew the facile secret of their creation. Like piecework I rolled them off" (151). She acknowledges, "Never, never did I soar on the wings of inspiration; the lines I wrote ... were painstakingly assembled, an artificial montage of poetic parts." She admits, "I was a literary conman, a quack, and the size of my early success was amazing, thrilling, and frightening" (152). Although Shields includes Charleen's comments on contemporary poetry, she does not include any of her poems, as she does in *Swann* (1987).

Shields recalls that, when she introduced her husband-to-be, Don Shields – a Canadian student whom she met while pursuing a study year abroad in Exeter, England – to her mother, she exhorted him to encourage Carol to continue her writing. He replied, "Her what?" since Carol had not mentioned to him that she wrote, suggesting that she was shy about her writing (*RI* 35). Don Shields, later professor and dean of engineering at the University of Manitoba in Winnipeg, proved very supportive of Carol's writing and continues to champion his late wife's work.

Marriage at twenty-two, followed by the birth of five children, stifled Shields's poetic voice for several years, although she admits to "reading a little poetry on the sly."[9] Eventually, inspired by the "honesty" of Philip Larkin's poetry, "a wonderful revelation" (*RI* 36), she began writing poetry again. Larkin was a major influence in the revival of Shields's poetic career: after seeing glowing reviews of his new collection, she read *The Whitsun Weddings* and *The Less Deceived* (Wachtel, 1989, 21) and realized, "'Good heavens, this man is being honest.' It really was a wonderful revelation" (*RI* 36). Larkin was a leader of "The Movement," a group of poets that rebelled against the pretentiousness of some Modernist poets and the excessive rhetoric of Dylan Thomas and the Poets of the Apocalypse in postwar Britain, and tried to establish an understated, colloquial poetry more reminiscent of *Lyrical Ballads* (1798) by William Wordsworth and Samuel Taylor Coleridge. Alex Ramon compares Shields's "direct address – accessible, unadorned language, concentrated form ... and an emphasis on the familiar over the allusive or abstruse" – to Larkin's poetic style, calling her verse "Larkinesque" (24–5).[10] She affirms, "I was amazed. I loved it. I'd read Eliot and Pound and so on in university, and modern poetry had disappointed me" (Wachtel, 1989, 21).

After reading Larkin's work, Shields determined, "'I'm going to write some poetry'" (RI 36). Motivated by a 1964 CBC competition for poets under thirty, Shields, who was then twenty-nine years of age, began writing poetry again. In her essay "A Sense of Place," she recalls, "acting out of obstinacy ... and also out of a conviction that all relationships are complex, even those of the suburban middle class, I sat down one dark Toronto winter in 1964 to write a group of poems about children, neighbours, my mother and sister, aunts and uncles and other ... so-called ordinary people, whatever that means. Eventually these poems appeared in a book titled *Others*" (Carol Shields Fonds, Accession 1994–13, Box 63, F 10, 15, LAC, quoted by Ramon 23). She won the competition.

Clearly, that hiatus of several years effected a significant development in Shields's poetic style. Marriage and motherhood, combined with her immigration to Canada and living abroad in England, inspired a different style of poetry from the conventional verse she had written as a girl. Positive reviews of *Others* confirm her success: Levenson, for example, asserts, "This is an exciting first book, and its effect is immediate" (Carol Shields Fonds, Accession 1994–13, Box 20, LAC).

Larkin helped revolutionize Shields's poetic method: "Larkin led me into this sort of perspective. When I finished a poem, I would ask myself the question – and this was something I had never done in my writing before – Is this what I really mean? I was very severe about it. I worked; when I think of the hours I spent revising and getting it just right, it gave me such pleasure" (RI 37–8). She adds, "There was a second question too: does this poem contain an idea? I knew I didn't want to write poems out of the lint of unfocused feeling ... I wanted to make hard, honest, thoughtful poems like those I had discovered by Philip Larkin" (De Roo 40). She affirms, "I was very strict with myself. I followed Larkin's set of rules: no pretty language" (RI 37). Anne Giardini recalls in "Freight Cars and Clotheslines and a Mother's Advice" that her mother said, "At the end of each poem I asked myself 'Is this what I really mean?' and it was the first time I took myself seriously ... I put that question to myself very sternly, and it often resulted in the rewriting of a poem to make sure I said what I really meant" (*Globe and Mail*, 24 March 2009). In *The Vortex*, Shields's first, unpublished, novel, Maude, the protagonist and editor of a poetry journal, declares, "words must convey meaning and not just jingle noisily like a pocketful of change" (Carol Shields Fonds, Accession 1994–13, Box 23, File 1, 44, LAC, quoted in Ramon 24).

Composing poems was more practical than writing novels for a mother of five. She recalls, "All spring, I had this little baby crawling around, and I wrote seven poems. I hadn't written poetry since those sonnets in high school. I worked and worked on those poems. It was the first time in my life that I took my writing seriously. In fact, I mailed them off the day before the deadline." She returned from the mailbox to hear her husband say, "Well it's nice to have you with us again." She adds, "They're all in my first book. One of them is about my son John, something he said; they were anecdotal" (Wachtel, 1989, 21). Robert Weaver, the renowned CBC Radio producer, telephoned to say that she had won the competition: "We're really pleased because none of us has ever heard of you" (*RI* 37), he remarked.

That catalyzed "an enormously happy" five-year period of composing poetry. Shields often claims that "Art is making." She recalls, "I was, for about five years, enchanted with the making of these little 'things.' (I remember once reading an essay by Gary Geddes in which he called poems 'little toys' one carries around in the head, and that is exactly what I felt.) It was exhilarating. I don't think I ever wrote with such giddy elation or revised with so much ardour" (De Roo 40). She affirms, "I felt as though I was making these lovely little things, these little toys" (Wachtel, 1989, 22).

In *The Stone Diaries* (1993) Shields asks, "How does a poet know when a poem is ended? Because it lies flat, taut; nothing can be added or subtracted" (71). She told an interviewer, "Writing poetry is a wonderful thing because you can sometimes get a poem perfectly." "After writing," she advises students in her essay "Be Bold All the Way Through," "ask yourself, 'Is this what I really mean?'" (*SI* 143).

In "Segue," Jane Sexton refers to her sonnet writing, somewhat ironically, as "my miniature art." Shields was occasionally considered a miniaturist – celebrated as a "Goddess of small things" by Mark Honigsbaum in the *Guardian* (23 May 1998, 6–7), for example. Shields viewed her poetry in a similar light: "I loved being a poet. I think partly because a poem is such a small thing. I always think of it as a kind of toy. You can get it almost right, and you can never get a novel almost right because a novel is just too big. There are just too many little parts to it, too many twigs and leaflets. But a poem you can get just about right."[11] Referring to her poetry as her miniature art reflects her view of her poems as *toys*, and, indeed, many of them do constitute miniature narratives, but the phrase "miniature art" may also refer to the belittling of her work by certain critics. The phrase formed part of the original title of this edition, but, after one reader responded, "This 'miniature art' is huge," I decided to omit it.

Shields recalls, "I'd had my fifth child, and she was going half-days to school. I just had a little bit of time, and I was writing poetry in those days. I was very interested in poetry for about five years, in reading it and writing it. And eventually – these were just published in small magazines in Canada" – including the *Antigonish Review, Arc, Books in Canada, Border Crossings, Canadian Forum, Fiddlehead, Quarry*, and *SALT*.[12] Her master's thesis supervisor at the University of Ottawa, Dr Lorraine McMullen, said, "'Well, look, we're in the publishing business. If you have fifty poems, we will publish a book.' So that, in fact, is what they did, and they published another book two years later," she recalls. "So I had the two books of poetry [*Others* and *Intersect*] before I sat down to write a novel."[13]

Initially, Shields submitted poems under the name "Ian McAllister," because she thought editors, mostly male, would be more likely to accept poems by a male poet. It worked. After Shields submitted (and had accepted) two items under this pen name, she wrote to Blanche Howard gleefully on 21 October 1983, "Ian (my pseudonym) has had 2 acceptances! Now *he* is a serious writer" (*MF* 56). (Note the initials of her pseudonym: "IM," a homonym for "I am.") Similarly, Margaret Laurence submitted poems to *The Manitoban* under the name "Steve Lancaster" – "after the Lancaster bomber," as she explains in *Dance on the Earth: A Memoir* (96). Margaret Atwood submitted poems under the gender-neutral moniker "M. Atwood," as a letter from McGill English professor and poet Louis Dudek, addressed to "Dear Mr. Atwood" and rejecting her submission to the journal *Delta*, confirms. She did employ the initials "M.E." for "Margaret Eleanor" at one stage. In *Negotiating with the Dead: A Writer on Writing* (2002), she explains, "I used my initials instead of a first name – I didn't want anyone important to know I was a girl" (21). In response to the question, "Who Do You Think You Are," the title of the opening chapter of *Negotiating with the Dead: A Writer on Writing*, she could reply honestly, "M.E."[14]

Shields's poetry clearly influenced her fiction writing, as many of her poems constitute miniature narratives. Alex Ramon considers the relationship of the poetry to her subsequent novels "particularly significant," as he observes "a notable amount of correlation in terms of style, form, and theme" (Ramon 22). Wiseman considers Shields "a superb prose writer, whose graduation from graceful comedies of manners to more ambitious narrative forms and deeper content has been rewarded by international recognition" (65). Shields affirms, however, "I never think of [poetry] now as apprenticeship for novel writing."[15] In comparing poetry to prose, she asserts, "poetry pops off in our heads like a flash bulb, prose like a steadily radiating incandescence" (De Roo 39). She explains, "It is really the way one word is placed surprisingly against another that sets off the flash, not verbal eccentricity" (*SI* 154).

Even if we did not have her work in other genres, however, Shields's poetry would be valued not only for its influence on her fiction, important as that is, but also for its own quality. Russell Smith affirms "the independent merit of her verse" (36), while Lee Anne Parpart labels her poems "wonders" because they "carry a tremendous power of their own" (17). "Shields demonstrates the power of her poetic vision"

(174), according to Mark Morton, and Levenson claims her poetry "manages, through a combination of striking imagery, unobtrusive rhyme and skillful line-breaks, to invest her own and our everyday world with unsuspected insights," which Morton labels *aperçus* or "ontological juxtapositions" (Morton 175).[16] In "Natural, Physical Simplicity," Joel Skuce claims Shields's poetry fulfills Louis Zukofsky's definition of poetry as "an order of words" that approaches "the wordless art of music." He argues that it creates the frisson that Robert Graves believed art should achieve (44). Wiseman affirms, "There is a lively grace about Carol Shields's best work, where the quilt of the poem is stitched perfectly" (67).

Peter Stevens judges that "Carol Shields has found a sure voice, approachable and yet revealing a subtle response to the ordinary and its underlying life" (Carol Shields Fonds, Accession 1994–13, Vol. 20, File 15, LAC). That *voice* influenced her subsequent fiction significantly, especially in the first-person narratives of her first two published novels, *Small Ceremonies* (1976) and *The Box Garden* (1977), published soon after her first two poetry collections. While some reviewers underestimated her range, deeming her work too focused on the domestic and ordinary, Morton praises "Shields's ability to transform the ordinary into something extraordinary" by her skillful "transformation of the mundane" (174), or what Shields's poet-protagonist Charleen Forrest calls in *The Box Garden* "my secret gift of alchemy" (152).[17] This is the feature of her writing that critics – from Adriana Trozzi's monograph *Carol Shields's Magic Wand: Turning the Ordinary into the Extraordinary* (2001) to Marta Dvořák and Manina Jones's edition *Carol Shields and the Extra-Ordinary* (2007) – have most admired. Atwood affirms, "It was the extraordinariness of ordinary people that was Shields's forte" (2004, 361).

Poetry also influenced and informed Shields's fiction even more directly, as poets figure prominently in certain novels. Charleen Forrest is a poet who claims "poetry became the means by which I saved my life" (*BG* 338). Mary Swann is a poet who was murdered and dismembered by her husband in *Swann* (1987), recalling British Columbia poet Pat Lowther, author of *A Stone Diary*, who was bludgeoned to death by her husband in 1975. In an ironic parallel, literary critics cannibalize Swann's image, until they are forced to reconstruct her vanishing poems, nineteen of which are included in the novel *and* in this collection.

Shields's poem "Emily Dickinson" illustrates her literary foremother's impact on Shields's own poetry as it foreshadows the cryptic quatrains of Mary Swann in *Swann*:

> Minutes hide their tiny Tears
> and Days weep into Aprons.
> A stifled Sorrow from the Years
> And Silence from the Eons (194)

This poem not only reflects Dickinson's own gnomic poems but is actually employed as one of Mary Swann's "*Swann Songs*" (*Swann* 48). Dickinson, like Larkin, was a major influence: her maxim, "Tell all the truth but tell it slant," provides the epigraph to *Various Miracles* (1985) – appropriately, for Shields's "sparkling subversion" (*SD* 337) is central to her oeuvre. Shields recalls "Emily Dickinson's insistence that a poem must take the top of her head off" (*SI* 21). In a review of *Others*, Levenson calls Shields's poetry "reminiscent at times of a married, and more stable, contemporary Emily Dickinson."[18]

Swann includes one of Shields's most eloquent celebrations of poetry, as her character, biographer Morton Jimroy, reflects, "When he thought of the revolution of planets, the emergence of species, the balance of mathematics, he could not see that any of these was more amazing than the impertinent human wish to reach into the sea of common language and extract from it the rich dark beautiful words that could be arranged in such a way that the unsayable might be said. Poetry was the prism that refracted all of life" (*Swann* 86). Shields also incorporates poetry into *A Celibate Season* (1991), the epistolary novel that she co-authored with Blanche Howard about a married couple separated for a season. Shields, who opted to write the letters from the husband, Charles, or "Chas," presents him taking a creative writing course called "Creative Connections" at Capilano College from Davina Flowering. Davina insists that "Poetry, if it's going to sing, has to be a slice right off the primordial soul ... Otherwise it's crap" (71). Chas composes poems that are included in the letters, including the lines "Each day now is an open mouth / heated with anger and yawning time" (66), while Howard, who wrote the letters from the wife, Jocelyn, or "Jock," presents her having an affair with a poet named Austin Grey and incorporates some of his poetry in her letters, including "I have wandered by night and seen black forms / And touched things colder than moonlight on a still spirit" from his book *Moonlight on a Still Spirit* (69).

Poetry influenced Shields's prose fiction in more general ways, however: her early work in poetry perfected her control of language. Clara Thomas opines, "Carol is the most word-enchanted novelist we have" (Levin 15), and Penelope Lively declares, "you are struck by the elegance of the writing – that wonderfully accurate dialogue, the apt phrases that shine out on every page" (xxxiii). Jay Parini exudes, "Her words ring like stones in a brook, chilled and perfected; the syntax rushes like water, tumbling with the slight forward tilt that makes for narrative. The reader is caught in whirlpools and eddies, swirled, then launched farther down-stream" (65). Caught in "the entrapment of words" (*Happenstance* 154) and enmeshed in "the labyrinth of language" ("Narrative Hunger" 23), Shields affirms that she was "always involved with language, right from the beginning" (*RI* 31).

Shields advises her creative writing students to "avoid 'poetic' words, pretty words, archaic words." Instead, she advises them to "Use a thesaurus" as Sylvia Plath did (*SI* 142) and recommends that they read a few pages of a dictionary to "settle the mind," as she herself did. Her archived notes contain lists of unusual words such as "plenitude," "chitinous," and "percipience."

While Shields is adept at diction and poetic form, her forte is metaphor: Levenson affirms, "we find ample evidence of the gift for metaphor ... that characterizes most of her poetry" (xxv). Shields reflects, "There was such a thing as allegory, there was such a thing as metaphor, there were the rewarding riches of symbol and myth. There were layers and layers – infinite layers – of meaning" (*H* 42) in which she revels. Shields's daughter, "Margaret, Aged Four," for example, is "Locked into imagery / rare as algebra" (72).[19] In her author's introduction to her juvenilia in *Early Voices*, Shields confesses of "Co-operative Miracle" (18), "I feel sure there are some terrible metaphors in it, since I was taking a Creative Writing course and had just discovered the wonders of imagery" (9).

Shields believes "A poem should be a flash of a camera; some part of it goes off" (*SI* 142). That snapshot effect is mimicked in her imagery. In "Illuminating the Moment: Verbal Tableaux in Carol Shields' Poetry," the only substantial essay on Shields's poetry to date, excepting Levenson's excellent introduction, Katharine Nicholson Ings praises Shields's "ability to create visual moments of almost epiphanic clarity [in] verbal tableaux – pictures painted through language" (168). For example, "Rough Riders" recreates "Huddle-time," in which footballers "play at priests / locked in holy circles/ plotting death/ by numbers," as "their bums rough / out lunatic lily pads / on the comic green" (75). The epiphanic scene that concludes her first novel, *Small Ceremonies*, wherein her heroine sees a group of deaf people engaged in animated conversation, their hands gesticulating like flowers, like birds, "shaping a private alphabet of air" (178) in a pantomime of communication, illustrates her poetic vision perfectly, demonstrating how her skill in poetry translates to her prose fiction. Shields frequently rehearses an image in a poem as a prelude to developing it in a novel: for example, in "Being Happy – 1949," she defines "Happiness" as "the lucky pane of glass/ you carried about/ in your head" that shields "a raging cavity/ with no way out" (142). She opens *Unless* (2001) with this statement: "Happiness is the lucky pane of glass you carry in your head" (1).

Metaphor influenced the ideological, aesthetic, and formal content of her poetry. Her verbal tableaux, which transform the ordinary into the extraordinary, may reflect the influence of photography and the Modernist Imagistes.[20] Her epiphanic imagery transforms the mundane into the miraculous, recreating "numinous moments," like the eternal moment that the Modernists captured, "random illuminations" that realize the spiritual in the actual.[21] She explains, "I have always been compelled, and comforted, too, by the idea of the transcendental moment, that each of us is allotted a few random instances in which we are able to glimpse a kind of pattern in the universe. All of my books, I think, *even the early books of poetry*, try to isolate and examine those odd, inexplicable moments. The accidental particles of our lives, for instance, suddenly align themselves, bringing about illumination, clarity, revelation, or extraordinary coincidence – which are in themselves reaffirming" (my emphasis, De Roo 46). She asks, "What is one to do with such moments? We seldom speak of them for fear of being misunderstood, and I am told that our language is poor in the kind of vocabulary these events demand. Nevertheless they must be paid attention to. They are, as my title [*Various Miracles*] suggests, miracles" (De Roo 46). Aritha van Herk affirms, "The real miracle is that there are miracles. And Carol Shields stories this wonder" (108).

A sense of the miraculous is a hallmark of Shields's writing, whether in poetry or prose. "Daddy" reveals the father as a magician who "rescued the spoiled air/ with rainbows" (126).[22] Many texts, both poetic and prosaic, build to a transcendent moment. Levenson admires the "spiritual poise" of her "framework of moral awareness" (cc xvix). Her poems, stories, and novels all strive to achieve that "moment of grace," as she phrases it in *Unless* (44), that realizes the extraordinary in the ordinary. She notes Browning's phrase "everlasting moment," that moment when things come together, which she refers to as "numinous moments," "moments of transcendence," or "random illuminations." She affirms, "I believe in these moments when we feel or sense the order of the universe beneath the daily chaos. They're like a great gift of happiness that comes unexpectedly" (*RI* 17).²³ She explains, "I'm not religious, though I was brought up in the Methodist Church and for a while I went to Quaker meetings. I do believe in these moments, though I don't know where that belief comes from. Not from any spiritual centre. I think it comes from the accidental *collision* of certain events" (*RI* 47).

Shields considers that "the English language is very poor in its vocabulary to describe mysticism, so a lot of this never gets talked about. Or only clumsily, or only by people that we think are perhaps only marginally sane. Or it's sometimes discoverable through poetry" (*RI* 47). She explains, "I think it's more of a celebration. When you experience one of those moments, it's like a great gift of happiness" (*RI* 47–8). Blanche Howard records that Shields, when she was dying of cancer, "spoke of how she cherished flashes of transcendence each day and how their radiance lit for a time the path she must follow" (*MF* 408).

In her essay "Narrative Hunger and the Overflowing Cupboard," she admits, "words, words alone, will always fail in their attempt to express what we mean by reality" (23). She adds, "But we must be able to recognize them and have the vocabulary to discuss them." In two of the last poems in *Intersect*, she expresses that miraculous experience with economy. In "Boy Waking Up" she writes, "by accident / the whole realm / of existence slid / into view for one / moment" (57), the final enjambment conveying the boy's breathless amazement. In "Carolers: Ontario" she imagines singers celebrating the nativity by "feeling their way / back toward the exact / centre where history / and miracle intersect / announcing another beginning" (114), as birth is created by the union of history and miracle.

The importance of metaphor to Shields's fiction, illustrated by stones and flowers in *The Stone Diaries* (1993), Fay McLeod's mermaids in *The Republic of Love* (1992), and Larry Weller's mazes in *Larry's Party* (1997), for example, can hardly be overestimated. Though fond of imagery, Shields is suspicious of symbolism. She recalls a writer who remarked, upon finishing a novel, "I just have to go back and put in the symbols."

She herself remarked of the symbols in *The Box Garden*, "Oh, I just stuck those in at the end" (Goertz 233). In fact, Shields usually integrates her symbolism into her fiction organically, making limestone the building material of *The Stone Diaries*, Fay McLeod a researcher of mermaids, and Larry Weller a creator of garden mazes.

Shields is wary of the pretentious symbolism that Modernist poets favoured, declaring, "I hate imposed symbolism." She wonders, "Who said symbols are the fleas of literature?" (Thomas 60). Charleen Forrest is scathing on the subject: "symbolism is such an impertinence, the sort of thing the 'pome' people might contrive. God knows how easily it's manufactured by those who turn themselves into continually operating sensitivity machines." She adds, "Of course, symbols have their uses. But something ties me to the heaviness of facts, the mysterious facts of existence" (*BG* 60). Unable to write poetry, having drained the well of her psyche, she reflects, "The only other alternative would be to join that corps of half-poets, those woozy would-bes who warble away in private obscurities, the band of poets that I've come to think of, in my private lexicon, as 'the pome people.'" Rejecting the "inner life," she believes "The poet has to report on surfaces, on the flower in the crannied wall, on coffee spoons and peaches,"[24] a rusted key discovered in the grass" (110). She admits of "the pome people," "They can be charming; they can be seductive, but long ago I decided to stop writing if I found myself becoming one of them" (21). Shields also prefers facts, eschewing the blatantly symbolic.[25]

Simon Leigh praises Shields's poetic expertise: "Tinkling clearly like crystal, the small, polished items of her experience are presented with such technical skill." He concludes simply, "This is rewarding work" (130). Shields's control of poetics, while skillful, is unobtrusive: she makes extensive use of rhyme, but so subtly that it is almost imperceptible, as reviewers never mention it. Peter Stevens praises Shields's "unusually effective rhyme schemes that rarely draw attention to themselves, adding an epigrammatic emphasis."[26] "The idea of rhyme in poetry comes out of prayer, incantations, ringing bells, hands clapping," Shields explains (*SI* 144).[27] The opening poem in her first collection, *Others*, for example, ends every line with a rhyming word, forming quatrains, but the rhyme is concealed by caesura and enjambment, creating a conversational quality. She gradually conceals her rhymes further by employing internal rhyme rather than end-rhyme, and half-rhyme rather than full rhyme. Eventually, she makes less use of rhyme, employing assonance and alliteration instead to create musicality. In "Betty," the tulip petals reveal "the remembering ridge / of origin" (88), and "Catherine" concludes with "mysteries match and meet" (*O* 56).

Shields limits her use of punctuation, instead employing spacing to punctuate poems: "line breaks and space do the work [in poetry] that punctuation does in prose. Periods and commas mostly come up like clutter in poems" (*SI* 152). In *Happenstance* (1980) she describes an Escher print of seagulls: "It was a puzzle, a spatial question mark. There was a balance, she sensed, some mystery, precision, and something ironic too about the relationship between those birds and the small, airy, but distinct spaces that separated them" (83). This analysis could serve as a description of Shields's artful use of space in her poetry.

Shields believes that "Poetry hands people an experience they've had but haven't articulated" (*SI* 142). She advises, "you want your reader to say, 'Ah hah, I've felt exactly that way, too, but I've never seen it articulated'" (*SI* 152).[28] Therefore, she prefers "poetry that is immediately accessible," that contains a truth but also "has a sub-text that arrives a moment later."[29] The accessibility of her poems is facilitated by their brevity and wit. Indeed, most of Shields's poems are quite short, usually well under one page. In "Reading My Mother," her daughter Anne expresses admiration for "the wit and spirit of her poetry" (12). "Poetry," Shields affirms, "needs to be terse, elliptical, allusive" (*SI* 154). Most poems conclude with a strong sense of closure,[30] like a punch line, for "wit relishes brevity, elegance, consciousness," as Levenson observes (xvii). Russell Smith agrees that the elegance of Shields's poetry "derives from its wit and brevity" (Carol Shields Fonds, Accession 1994–13, Vol. 20, File 17, LAC).

With *Coming to Canada*, Shields's range gradually extends in time and space, as her developing persona situates memories in "the slow unfolded history / of our own green / earth" in "Love – Age 20" (147) and "Pioneers: Southeast Ontario," while reaching further afield geographically from America to Canada. Shields majored in English and history at Hanover, and her assertion in "Confession," "time's tenanted chronicle / fills me full" (64), reflects her interest in the past. As Wiseman claims in his review of *Coming to Canada*, "The dominant subject-matter of this collection is the recollection and examination of moments which have knitted a life together" (68).

Within "the arc of a human life," Shields emphasizes love and marriage – "the *leitmotif* of love, so central to her fiction," as Levenson phrases it (xxii). Although, as Anne Giardini claims in "The Square Root of a Clock Tick: Time and Timing in Carol Shields's Poetry and Prose," "the word 'love' is entirely missing from *Others* and *Intersect*" (27), love is highlighted in *Coming to Canada*. "Love – Age 20" celebrates the "unearned gift of / love" (148). The final poem in *Coming to Canada* is "Coming to Canada – Age Twenty-Two," when Shields crossed the forty-ninth parallel with her husband in 1957, with her ironing board stowed in their old Ford. The poet's persona recalls Aunt Violet's postcard from her 1932 Canadian honeymoon, reading "COME BACK SOON." But the speaker observes that, eventually,

> COME BACK SOON changed to
> here and now and home
> the place I came to
> the place I was from. (150)[31]

The difference between *to* and *from* is crucial to this poem *and* to the entire collection.

Given the appeal of Shields's poetry and its positive reception by reviewers, one wonders why it has been largely ignored subsequently by scholars, critics, jurors, and anthologists. There are several possible reasons for this relative neglect. The most obvious is the fact that Shields's poetry has been overshadowed by her famous fiction. Other recent Canadian women authors who began their literary careers as poets and went on to publish fiction, such as Margaret Atwood and Jane Urquhart, also found their early poetry overshadowed by their fiction.[32] Female authors were also often dismissed as "women writers" and their emphasis on the domestic viewed as trivial.[33] For example, in "All Plot, Little Thought," Robert Lecker dismisses Shields's first novel, *Small Ceremonies*, as "a reasonably entertaining story about the significant trivialities of everyday suburban existence," in which "nothing particularly exciting happens" (80), although it later won the Canadian Authors Association Award for the best novel of 1976. Shields, however, believes in the value of the domestic life. In her essay "Arriving Late: Starting Over" she asks, "Why had domesticity, the shaggy beast that eats up ninety percent of our lives, been shoved aside by fiction writers?" (247). Lorraine York notes Shields's frustration at being labelled "the poet of the prosaic, the bard of the banal" (238). She quotes Atwood's comment that Shields was not taken seriously because she was "cute, short, and blond" (248). Shields's daughter observes, "at five foot two, eyes of blue," she was "the very image of a middle-class American teenage girl in the middle of the last century (Giardini 2014, 26–7). Atwood affirms of Shields, "She knew about the darkness, but – both as an author and as a person – she held onto the light ... Earlier in her writing career, some critics mistook this quality of light in her for lightness, light-mindedness, on the general principle that comedy ... is less serious than tragedy, and that the personal life is of less importance than the public one. Carol Shields knew better" (2004, 360). In her foreword to *Startle and Illuminate*, Jane Urquhart reflects, "She was as fascinated by the dark as she was by the light. In these pages she explores the sun and the shadows of the writing life" (xii).

Canadian women poets tended to compose confessional poetry in the late twentieth century, while Shields eschewed such introspective verse, avoiding "anything that could be construed as confessional" (Levenson xvii) and focusing more on observation.[34] Moreover, her poetry is understated, rejecting the intellectualism of some Modernist poets, and hence easily dismissed as superficial. In "Parties Real and Otherwise," Shields explains to an interviewer, "The poems in the early two books were, as you say, about 'others.' One of my mentors, Chris Levenson, used to ask me when I was going to 'come out' and write from the 'I' posture. My own sense was that those early poems were all filtered through my 'I' and were as personal as those that came later."[35] Levenson affirms, "Mrs Shields' habitual stance is one of wry, critical, but sympathetic detachment," but concludes, "It is to be hoped that when she comes to deal more directly with her first person experiences she will do so with the same vivacity and wit" (Carol Shields Fonds, Accession 1994–13, Vol. 20, File 15, LAC).

Whereas a few female critics disapprove of her restraint and lack of explicit feminism, most male reviewers approve of Shields's avoidance of the overly personal and confessional. Peter Stevens commends her for "avoiding the too private tone, the too confessional posturing that can mar poetry of this nature" (Carol Shields Fonds, Accession 1994–13, Vol. 20, File 15, LAC); Simon Leigh observes that "Carol Shields' horror of overstatement keeps her effects small, polishing, working to avoid being trite" (130); Michael Brian Oliver, reviewing various female poets, observes "an inordinate preponderance of female Hamlets" and approves the fact that Shields "is not lost in herself" (37–8); Wiseman praises her "confident, well-structured, sophisticated poems" with their "quiet celebration" of the "small ceremonies in life" (69); and W.J. Keith concludes, "Carol Shields is modest, unassuming, quietly competent ... with a subtle combination of distanced irony and genuine affection ... This is an unostentatious verse that avoids the grand statement but can often startle with sharp insight" (3192).

Shields prefers objectivity and frequently adopts a novelist's stance, not only in her fiction but also in her poetry, as she does in her poem "I/Myself" (123), which contrasts frames of subjectivity. She could speak more openly through the mask of the fictional characters of her novels, as we see in Reta Winter's angry unsent letters in *Unless*, compared to the first-person personae of her poems. In *Small Ceremonies*, her protagonist-narrator, Judith Gill, reports of a disturbing event, "I can live outside it. I can outline it with my magic pencil. Put a ring around it" (*SC* 124). Thus, writing poetry may have proved therapeutic or cathartic for Carol Shields. In her afterword to *Dropped Threads 2*, she explains how she dealt with a hurt done to her by a senior male colleague by burying it in *The Stone Diaries*.

As a young mother of five children, Shields was not part of the poetry-reading scene, so crucial to being recognized as a poet.[36] Atwood recalls Shields saying, while she was living in Toronto in the sixties, an era Atwood characterizes as "a time of poetic ferment in that city" (2004, 361), that she did not know any writers. Living in Ottawa during the seventies, when her first two books of poetry were published, she was also occupied with completing her master's degree in Canadian literature. Although winning the Pulitzer Prize and the Governor General's Award for Fiction for *The Stone Diaries* (1993) catalyzed attention to Shields's subsequent fiction, including *Larry's Party* (1997) and *Unless* (2001), the fact that her poetry collections, along with her first four published novels, predated that watershed led to their continued neglect.[37]

In the influential 1983 *Oxford Companion to Canadian Literature*, Constance Rooke damns Shields's verse with faint praise, judging, "Shields's poetry is less impressive than her fiction, although marked by the same appealing sensibility. The poems are simple, domestic, generous in spirit, though often technically undistinguished. Our satisfaction typically comes in the moment of insight" (Rooke 752).[38] That climactic "moment of insight," praised by Keith, Oliver, and others, is, of course, what distinguishes Shields's poems.

Although Shields won numerous awards, eventually she suffered from "the Munro Doctrine," a pun on the Monroe doctrine, named for Alice Munro, whereby the author is shot into the stratosphere far beyond the ken of jurists, as Atwood affirms (2004, 361). The fact that most editors and reviewers were male was a factor, although other female poets of the era – including Gwendolyn McEwen, P.K. Page, Margaret Atwood, Dorothy Livesay, Elizabeth Brewster, and Phyllis Webb – received greater respect for their poetry than Shields did, perhaps because their work was more deeply personal or more explicitly feminist.

Feminism may well have been a factor, as Shields's early writing, while implicitly feminist, is not explicitly so. Laura Groening takes exception, in an article titled "Still in the Kitchen," to Shields being called a feminist in the sense that Betty Friedan delineates in *The Feminine Mystique* (1963). Growing up in the postwar period when American women were hustled back into the kitchen and bedroom, Shields frequently acknowledged, in essays such as "Arriving Late: Starting Over," coming late to feminism. She lamented to me in May 2003, "I think I was the last feminist to wake up in the world."[39] But reviewing her early novels and first two poetry collections in light of her later novels reveals the implicit feminism that eventually becomes explicit in Reta Winters's angry (unsent) letters, as she finds the courage to "blurt it all out" (*Unless* 270). In various poems Shields expresses the "rage" of Aunt Violet and Aunt Ada, plus the "anger" and "rage" of "golden-agers" (133, 138, 186), revealing the indignation and outrage of that neglected generation of women, such as Daisy Goodwill of *The Stone Diaries*, whom Shields was at pains to "redeem."

Shields's subversive feminism surfaces in "Voices," which concludes with a vivid image suggesting repressed rage:

a Chinese lady's shoe
screaming
in a glass case. (161)

Atwood reflects, "Possibly feminism was something she worked into, as she published more widely and came up against more commentators who thought excellent pastry was a facile creation compared to raw meat on skewers, and who in any case could not recognize the thread of blood in her work, though it was always there" (2004, 363). As Atwood observes, Shields's first four books – two poetry collections and two novels, published in the seventies, "the decade of rampant feminism" – "examined the vagaries of domestic life without torpedoing it" (362), and hence did not make waves among second-wave feminists. Second-wave feminism could also account for the paucity of female reviewers of Shields's poetry, although male reviewers, like editors, predominated in the early seventies.[40] Atwood observes, "[Shields] understood the life of the obscure and the overlooked partly because she had lived it. Her study of Jane Austen reveals a deep sympathy with the plight of the woman novelist toiling incognito, appreciated only by an immediate circle but longing for her due" (2004, 361). Lorraine York traces the phenomenon of Shields's literary celebrity astutely in "'Arriving Late as Always': The Literary Celebrity of Carol Shields," concluding, "it is much to Shields's credit that she used her star power both wisely and generously" (252). Shields's poetic style may not have been particularly fashionable in the late twentieth century, but now, in the twenty-first century, we can appreciate its appeal anew. It is hoped that this collection of her complete poetry may inspire a renewed appreciation of Shields's work.

Although Carol Shields died before she could complete her novel about the sonneteer, Atwood wrote in her tribute to her, "And live she did, and live she does. For, as John Keats remarked, every writer has two souls, an earthly one and one that lives on in the world of writing as a voice in the writing itself. It's this voice, astute, compassionate, observant and deeply human, that will continue to speak to her readers everywhere" (2004, 363).

NOTES

1. Professors Frank Tierney and Glenn Clever of the University of Ottawa Department of English founded Borealis Press in 1972.
2. Shields noted this in a 1998 interview for the American Academy of Achievement, https://www.carol-shields.com/biography.html.
3. Upon graduating from Hanover College in 1957, Carol Shields was slated to win the writing prize, but was asked if she would agree to cede the prize to the second-place student, since he was a man and would have to have a good career in order to support a family. She agreed (*SI* xxii).
4. "Sonnet" is on page 260 of this edition. Unless otherwise specified, all parenthetical page references for poems, except for "Catherine" and poems from *Early Voices*, are to this edition.
5. Shields's daughter, published poet Sara Cassidy, revised "Moment's Moment" as "Segue" for *The Collected Stories* (2003). The front of the dust cover announces, "Featuring 'Segue,' a previously unpublished story."
6. For a fuller discussion of this work, please see my essay "'Fragments on My Apple': Carol Shields's Unfinished Novel" and my interview with Shields, "'Excursions into the Sublime': A Personal Reminiscence of Carol Shields."
7. Although Shields wrote her MA thesis on the novels of Canadian pioneer writer Susanna Moodie, she had planned to write it on Canadian poet P.K Page. She records, "I was going to do P.K. Page because I liked her poetry. I even interviewed her when she was in Ottawa, staying at the Chateau Laurier" (Wachtel, 1989, 24).
8. While most of her juvenilia published in *Early Voices* are omitted from this edition at the request of her family, a few poems published in her university magazine when she was aged twenty-two – including "Sonnet," "Mark Twain," and "Napoleon at St. Helena" – are included since they are not, strictly speaking, "juvenilia," which normally refers to works written before the age of twenty.
9. Shields made this comment in an unpublished 1990 convocation address at the University of Ottawa.
10. Although Ramon discusses Shields's first two poetry collections, *Others* (1972) and *Intersect* (1974), he does not address her third collection, *Coming to Canada* (1992).
11. Shields's 1998 interview for the Academy of Achievement.
12. Peter Stevens published several of Shields's poems as editor of *Forum*, but eventually suggested other magazines to her (Wachtel, 1989, 23).
13. Shields recalled this in a 1 May 2002 interview with Terry Gross on Public Radio. Don Shields recalls that Glenn Clever, the head of the English Department, invited Carol to write a collection of poems that Borealis would publish. She agreed.
14. In her 2007 lecture on Margaret Laurence, published in 2011 in "Margaret Atwood," *A Writer's Life: The Margaret Laurence Lectures*, Atwood calls the period in question "a literary world in which it was commonplace to say that women couldn't write, and neither could Canadians, and any woman or any Canadian who tried was likely to meet more than one big slap-down" (215).
15. In a 1998 interview for the Academy of Achievement.

16 Carol Shields's agent Bella Pomer claims, "Carol's an exquisite writer with a sensibility for the uniqueness of the ordinary, although she's open to experimental and fanciful stories too" (Levin 15).
17 Morton thinks Skuce underestimates Shields's poetry in this manner, but Skuce's review of *Coming to Canada* is complimentary, arguing that her poems demonstrate that ordinary experience can prove epiphanic.
18 Levenson's review of *Others* is in the file labelled "Others" Reviews in Carol Shields Fonds, Accession 1994–13, Box 20, p. 1, Library and Archives Canada (LAC).
19 Eric Thomson declared, "if fantasy is the life-blood of poetry – the poet's image-making faculty which nurtures and sustains his imagined view of himself and his experience of the world –[Carol Shields is a] fantasist, in a minor key" (101).
20 As Sarah Gamble observes, "it is the nature of epiphany to be ephemeral" (46).
21 Shields's phrase "random illuminations" provided the title for Eleanor Wachtel's book.
22 The typescript of "Daddy" concludes with the word "rainbow," although the final line, "Of all things," was inserted in pencil beneath.
23 It is no coincidence that the working title of her final, unfinished novel was "A Moment's Moment," although it is crossed out and the title "Segue" is written underneath.
24 The mention of "coffee spoons and peaches" is a reference to T.S. Eliot's 1917 dramatic monologue "The Love Song of J. Alfred Prufrock."
25 Dee Goertz remarks that *The Box Garden* reveals that Shields was thinking about symbolism as early as 1977, suggesting that even scholars of Shields's work are sometimes unaware that she published two books of poetry containing over one hundred poems in all before ever publishing a novel.
26 Peter Stevens, "Poets and the Courage of the Ordinary," review of *Others*, *Globe and Mail*, 28 July 1973 (Carol Shields Fonds, Accession 1994–13, Vol. 20, File 15, LAC).
27 Shields asks in her archived notes, "What is poetry, Primitive form. A prayer or incantation, before story-telling, a directness that goes beyond story-telling. Normally has more concentrated power – due to images, ellipsis, foregoing formal structure, punctuation or syntax; rhythm, rhyme" (Carol Shields Fonds, Accession 2003–09, Box 92, File 9, LAC).
28 Shields states in archived notes for a creative writing course, "Poem wants you to say Ahah, rather than tell a story, suggest rather than lay it on you" (Carol Shields Fonds, Accession 2003–09, Box 92, File 9, LAC).
29 Shields is quoted in an unnamed and undated clipping in the Carol Shields Fonds of a review of *Coming to Canada* in the *Toronto Star*. The reviewer claims Shields's accessibility is "strongly reminiscent of the verse of the late British poet Philip Larkin."
30 Shields affirms, "The feeling of completion, however imperfect, is what makes art" (*SI* 19).

31 The Carol Shields Fonds, Accession 2003–09, Box 114, File 5, LAC, contains the missing penultimate verse for the final poem of the collection *Coming to Canada*:

> This love is lost in the snow
>   and the winter is gone
> Instead of come back soon
>   There is the sharpness of now.

32 Levenson affirms, "fiction [is] so much more visible than poetry in our society" (xi).
33 Shields acknowledges, "I'm puzzled and irritated by the notion that the domestic is peripheral. The home is a place of rest and acceptance. It's central to my own yearnings" (Levin 16).
34 In "Scream: New Canadian Women Poets," Michael Brian Oliver laments the "inordinate preponderance of female Hamlets" (38), but finds Carol Shields's *Others* a "notable exception" (37) that offers "unique insights" instead of soul-searching. Ramon labels Shields's verse "a poetry of observation, concerned to offer 'reportage' on neglected 'everyday' subjects" (23) with its emphasis on perception and observation and its "implicit suspicion of interiority" (25).
35 In *Small Ceremonies*, Shields's protagonist, Judith Gill, states, "my sister Charleen [protagonist of *The Box Garden*] writes and publishes poems of terrifying bitterness" (124).
36 Carol Shields's husband, Don Shields, wrote to me saying, "Carol probably did not talk up her poetry much. She was indeed a mother of young children at the time when the original poetry books were published, and she was working on an M.A. in English."
37 While *The Republic of Love* sold a respectable 3,000 copies in hard cover, *The Stone Diaries*, after winning the Pulitzer Prize, sold 10,000 copies in four days (Levin 15).
38 Although Patricia Irwin includes material on Shields's subsequent publications in the revised edition of the *Oxford Companion to Canadian Literature*, she does not address Shields's subsequent collection of poetry, *Coming to Canada* (1992, 1995).
39 Shields acknowledges this in my interview with her, "'Excursions into the Sublime': A Personal Reminiscence of Carol Shields."
40 Don Shields observes that, in that era, "men poets were dominant, as were men editors of poetry magazines. Men were also the poetry editors of general magazines."

THE COLLECTED POETRY OF CAROL SHIELDS

Others, Intersect, and *Coming to Canada*

SHIELDS'S FIRST THREE poetry collections contain 163 poems in all: *Others*, published by Borealis Press in 1972, contains fifty-one poems; *Intersect*, also published by Borealis Press in 1974, includes fifty poems; and *Coming to Canada*, published by Carleton University Press in 1992, collects seventy-nine poems in all – twenty-four under the heading *Coming to Canada* and eleven from each of the first two collections, plus thirty-eight "New Poems" drawn from her "Sunday Poems" and "Time Line" series. This collection was republished following the success of Shields's 1993 novel *The Stone Diaries*, which won the Pulitzer Prize in the United States and the Governor General's Award for Fiction in Canada. The first two editions have been out of print for decades.

The titles of Shields's three collections of poetry suggest their interrelationships. While *Others* contains poems exploring the mystery of difference, *Intersect* explores connections between self and other. As

Ings affirms, "Shields bridges the gap (one that is widely felt in the 1990s) between self and other" (172), continuing, "There is no outpouring of excess emotion, no sprawling lines, but a clean sparseness that matter-of-factly expresses both the familiar and the shocking" (173). In *Liminal Spaces: The Double Art of Carol Shields*, Alex Ramon considers Shields's interest in Self and Other Lacanian, claiming that her "abiding concern with existential aloneness and separation from the 'Other' means that Shields's work engages with concepts theorized by Jacques Lacan" in his 1973 study *The Four Fundamental Concepts of Psychoanalysis* (Ramon 21). *Coming to Canada* is essentially autobiographical, as the title suggests, as she immigrated to Canada from the United States when she married Canadian engineer Don Shields in 1957 at age twenty-two.

Carol Shields composed the poems in *Others* and *Intersect* while she was living in Ottawa from 1969 to 1975 and pursuing a master of arts in Canadian literature at the University of Ottawa, where she also taught courses in English literature and creative writing. She composed the new poems collected in *Coming to Canada* while she was living in Winnipeg, where she resided from 1981 to 1998 and where she served as professor of English at the University of Manitoba and chancellor of the University of Winnipeg.

OTHERS

Shields centres her study of *others* on the family, focusing on her five children. The family circle widens to include friends, acquaintances, and neighbours. Levenson suggests one section of *Others* could be titled "Neighbourhood Watch" (*CC* xvii).[1] While Levenson considers the focus on family verges on "stifling coziness," Ings disagrees: "in Shields's hands, this material transcends the sentimental" (168).

Observing "Others" involves awareness of their separateness, their mystery. In her essay "Where Curiosity Leads," Shields acknowledges, "What interested me ... was the *unknowability* of others, their very *otherness*, in fact. It was apparent to me that members of close, loving families resisted the forces of coercive revelation, and that even partners in long, happy marriages remained, ultimately, strangers, one to the other" (*si* 83). Poems such as "John," inspired by her eldest child, illustrate Shields's repeated comment in "Framing the Structure of a Novel": "What interested me ... was the *unknowability* of others, their very *otherness*, in fact" (26). In Shields's first novel, *Small Ceremonies*, her narrator, Judith Gill, a biographer, recognizes the ultimate mystery of her subject, Susanna Moodie, and even of her own family.

The novelist is already apparent in Shields's interest in *Others*: her portraits of "Daddy," "Grandma," and "Aunt Ada" could be sketches for the characters of a novel. The budding playwright is also apparent in her early poems, as she contrives to render them dramatic. She believes "There is one line that unwinds a poem" (*si* 142); for Shields, that line usually concludes the poem, as she uses closure for dramatic effect.

While *Others* focuses primarily on family, acquaintances, and neighbours, Shields does include some poems about herself,[2] although she often *others* herself, calling herself "she" or "someone," or dividing herself in two – the observer and the observed – as she does in her poem "I/Myself" (*cc* 6), and as Daisy Goodwill does in *The Stone Diaries*.

NOTES

1. In "Postcards from Home," a review of *Coming to Canada*, Anne Rayner judges that, like her fiction, Shields's poems "explore a poetics of suburbia" (Carol Shields Fonds, Accession 1994–13, Vol. 20, File 17, 197, LAC).
2. In "Female Poetry," her review of Shields's *Others*, Susan Zimmerman observes, "Most of the titles stress the 'otherness' of the people described, in contrast to the united 'we.' The effect is one of distance, irony. Yet the best of the poems are not about 'Others,' but about ourselves."

A Woman We Know Who Suffers from Occasional Depression

Afternoons collapse
when five o'clock frays
toward night, and days
launched in order, lapse
into riot.
    I housekeep
in rooms of my making, squares
of reason stacked against the clock.
Then darkness leaks like gas to block
the logic of supper, belief, prayers
and sleep.

The trick
is to find the square
root of a clock tick
and hide there.

Advice from a Green-Thumbed Friend

Slick as waxed water
this rubber plant
swallows up sun,
juicing its green breadth
in a pool of perfect light.

    Disregard its gross health,
    its porous good nature.
    Removed from this graced
    spot it would die in a matter
    of hours, its moist tongues
    torn out.

But watch the philodendron,
tendrilled beyond belief, sprout
precocious from a stringy throat,
insolent with bright
unnecessary growth.

    It out-snakes the future.
    It knows what it wants,
    root-room, leaf volume,
        space, it dreams of jungle space.

Margaret at Easter

From the choir she makes
angelic O's of song,
hosannas pumped from her seven-year lungs.

Already she's witnessed
the chocolate-marshmallow dawn,
been brought to this place and dressed
in redeeming white,

where the organ shakes
with the juice of holiness,
and Spring
like a flattened angel of air
presses down on this greening
roof and slips through the
tilted window to where
she sings
     behind the lilies,
     second from the right,
Hallelujah.

The Ferryman at Prince Edward County

Busy with his ropes and gears,
Tides and currents.
he didn't know and never
will how he came to appear
scowling in our
family snapshot.

We brought him home
by accident
on a film showing
part of a holiday,
children in jerseys on the dock,
grinning, puddled in sun,
and at the edge,
the ferryman's dark image.

Well, that's one way
to survive,
to be captured alive
by someone, caught
by a click and locked
in a box held by an unknown
hand at an unknown hour.

Later to rise from
a chemical bath imprinted on
a glossy three-by-five
to glare
out forever,
unknowing.

Some Old Friends Who Flew to England

From where we sat
over the wing, we saw
our shadow floating flat
on the waves like a flaw
on film, through the stirred
breath of weather, then blurred
in the first dark and drowned
without leaving a mark or a sound,

To pass the time we revived
that old argument,
which plane is real?

But it's a formal exercise
since we've already survived
so long in the brickwork,
growing middle-age wise
to these abstract quirks,

certain only of steel,
and knowing that planes meant
for drowning are for the drowned.

The New Mothers

Nearly seven,
walls loosen, it's already dark,
dinner trays rattle by,
nurses slack off, catch
a smoke, let go.
Roses bloom in every room.

Nearby
the egg-bald babies lie, stretching
pink like rows of knitting,
insects in cases, and cry
tiny metal tunes,
hairpins scratching
sky.

The mothers gather
together in clutches
of happy nylon,
brushing and brushing their hair.

They bunch at the frosted windows
in quilted trios
watching the parking lot where

pair after pair
the yellow headlights arc
through blowing snow –
the fathers
    are coming.

A Woman We Saw in an Antique Shop

The shop bell rings false
welcome, and hands touch table tops,
fingering the dark scars
hopefully; but there's no pulse
here and nothing to tell
anyway.

    Might as well
sell the black breath in old jars
or velvet dust from a chair crease
as clocks stopped on a wall.

Gloves poke the plates and cups,
wanting nothing, after all,
but a conversation piece.

A Cynical Friend Explains

For years the best kept secret of my childhood
was my power over the moon.
In the lane after supper I stood
in the thickening dark, and as soon
as the moon came up I put back
my head, and walking slowly in circles, could see
the strange, inexplicable fact,
the moon followed me.

Explanation came one soft summer night
as I whispered it all to my brother, leading
him to the lane so he might
see himself. But he interrupted pleading

that the moon followed him. So
back to back we paced off steps, he one way,
I the other. The moon, it seemed, could go
both ways at once. From that day

I relinquished magic, seeing in an instant
that, like the unconcerned sun,
the moon, distant
and democratic, followed everyone.

Anne at the Symphony

She listens like someone submitting
to surgery;
and at twelve she's quiet
under the knife,

stilled in ether, permitting
an alien clarinet
to scoop out an injury
we can't even imagine.

Jittery violins
devise a cure
and the vinegar pure
flutes doodle a theory
of life

which dissolves in
a memory of a memory
and bleeds like sand
through her faintly
clapping hands.

A Fiftyish Aunt

We like to think
of her as she was that night,
a fiftyish woman and heavy hipped,
in a kitchen rinsed
with milky light.

Something we said made her laugh,
and she turned from the sink
and the supper dishes, her elbows
flashing like flints,
and her wrists crocheted
with a winking line
of suds and tipped
with a broth of rainbows,
splitting her ancestral skin in half,

exposing a satin sachet
heart, a pink
new-minted
girlish valentine.

Grandpa Who Is Eighty at the Cottage

From the porch
he watched the carnival
coloured sun
come down,

its scorched
rays bent
like elbows
through the fretting trees,

filling up the country
windows
for miles around
with squares of light.

He knows
nothing of allegory
and was uncertain
at first what it meant

except that it was nearly night,
time to close
the beguiling curtains

and round off the ritual
so simply
begun.

A Husband Thinks Out Loud

In the garden riot of our first
married room with its iron bed
and bureau carved with leaves,

peonies burst
from the linoleum and crawled
up the trellised walls
where roses weaved
like drunkards through chenille.

You said
they must have blessed us with
their breath, their flat, unreal,
unscented, holy breath.

Insomniac

My midnight daydreams are crazed
by recollections which unwind
in the gothic dark like heresies,
cutting the nightscape in half.

Dipping and swimming the brain sees
whirling visions spun
from acute reality
        while the bare
electric bulb of nightmare
switches off and on.

Hourly I grow more over-defined
like a figure squared off on a graph,
advancing by rigid degrees
toward death
        until I find
myself eating   like grapes   the dazed
kilowatts of dawn.

Sara

After the supermarket my young
daughter rides home among
the groceries,
wound in a coffee-perfumed
paperbag cocoon.

She is outdistanced by celery.

There's no room
to move, and she cries
all the way home
as though stung
by mystery.

A Member of the Bridge Club

Hands around the table show blue veins
    and folded nylon legs declare
their unity. All afternoon they remain
    in their chairs, moving cards, thinking where
did it all start anyway. Over cake they speak
    of tricks lost, not that they care
much. Don't forget, my place next week.
    What else is there?

Michael
A Boy in Our Neighbourhood

Later he'll feel the earth's unending
indifference. Now he's climbing a tree,
one of those old-girlish willows bending
in space over water. I can see

by his touch on the rough intelligent turning
of the trunk that he believes
beyond all botany and learning
in the kindness of those leaves.

A Married Couple

      He

Once we touched above
    the hurting snow
    and our simple skins lit
    the interior of a universe.
Now we knit
    more intricate patterns of love,
    for better or for worse,
    you know and I know.

      She

You wear your bruise
on your face, exotic
star-shaped tattoo
of illness.
    I too,
in the secret
and unused
width of my heart,
have come apart.

Child Who Is Falling Asleep

Truly believing all other children
enter nightly into a pastel kingdom
of dreams, dense with
good fairies
and brave deeds,

he shifts and settles
in the sheeted trough
of his ever so spotless guilt,

listening for the flushed breath
of the furnace switching on,
lord of the chilly basement,

hearing the downstairs voices overcome
by thin teakettle
music, steaming the patterned kitchen.

The walls tilt
inward, shutting him off.
The nightlight leads
him back: he will always
be different.

An Old Lady We Saw

Before the ambulance came we covered
her with coats since it was cold
on the ice where she fell

and frightening where her hip
shot out surrealistically.

We saw her slip,
watched her go
down, heard the old
bones crack clean like a bell.

She should have cursed
the deceitful ice, the murderous cold,
not to mention our thinly gathered
concern, our clockwork sympathy.

Instead her needlepoint mouth moved, blue
against the oatmeal snow,
saying the wrong thing, the worst
thing, thank you, thank you.

Our Artist Friends

Sunday morning
early, twined warm
together in our polished
nest of sheets, we woke
to weather warnings,

an Old Testament storm
spilling out loud
from the mythic far-away
throat of Texas.

The wind shattered
our chowder sky, ravished
the widowed backyard elms,
                              kept us
in all day,
out of touch,
untalkative and shuttered
tight in the rain-bearded
house.

At six the clouds

rolled up like laundry,
the yellow yolk of sun poked
out and we cheered
from the window, astonished
to find it mattered
so much.

Our Old Aunt Who Is Now in a Retirement Home

Blinds shut out the bothering sun
    where Auntie lies, stewed
    in authentic age.

She has come unglued
    in her closet of brown breath
    and her memories
    tremble like jellies.

There's little to say.
    Awake
    she lives from tray to tray,
    briefly fingering
    squares of cake.

The final outrage,
    not death,
    but lingering
    has begun.

A Professor We Know Who Is a Compulsive Storyteller

He's shy and remote,
    but touch his fringed wits
    with a single word
    and like a tinderbox
he explodes with stories
    he's heard.

    He's intense
and amusing, serving up bits
    of history
    chopped into blocks,
    shaped in the candleglow
    and miniaturized
over coffee.

We're hypnotized
    and so is he
    by the Renaissance flow
    of his anecdotes.

They are his chief defense,
    his only jewelry.

Someone I Don't Like Anymore and Never Really Did

She was
a friend, but now we're on formal
terms, bridged with Christmas cards,
cozied with greetings.
I loathe her
and with cause.

For she is sadly missing the chromosome
of kindness and her blank bones
support the soul of a turnip.

Furthermore, envy clusters in her sour
heart like rhubarb though her anger
is relentlessly cordial.

Lately I've seen malice flower
from her shell-pink fingertips.

The Wesleyan Sunday School said I should love her.
The Freudian circle said I should be understanding.

But it's a glorious glory
at age thirty-six to afford
at last the luxury
of an unhealthy enmity.

No One's Simple, Not Even Sally

No one's simple, not even
Sally, balancing
on her own private meridian
of niceness, just a jot away
from the real thing,
goodness,

usually seen against
the household props, indentured
to small details, glistening
with appointments,

her face a landscape
of oval serenity.

At her house the air's
warmed by tea, the temperature
is just right, the roof shaped
for listening.

The oiled furniture
attends her,
and in the open
door a photographer
is waiting.

Someone We Met Who Grew Up on a Farm

Odd to see natural elements in the city.
Snow should be stuck on barns and hills,
not on assembly plants. And it seems a pity
to waste the rain. It only fills

the sewers up, at most creates
a driving hazard. The wind is stopped
by office blocks and weather waits
until the word is dropped

from the all-perceiving weather men
who allow no surprises. Warm and clear
tomorrow, they say solemnly, but then
even the sun is an alien shadow here.

Our Old Professor

Our old professor, a thorough man,
stunned a frog with an ether cloud
and stretched its foot on the stand
of a microscope,
                then allowed
us each to look in the miniature ring
at the snarl of thumping veins,

and never knew that the sight and shock
of blood cells moving slick as trains
along a track, unlocked
for a shuttered instant
the secret to everything.

Someone Hurrying Home

Hurrying home with my collar turned up
has made me separate. The snow
wetly caked to boot muffles steps, cups
me in quiet. I know

that looking up I'll meet
the tilting sleet. Better to keep eyes
on the frozen circle at my feet,
cut off. Even my breath lies
in separate clouds behind me, measuring off air.

Only the brain is alive, thinking on cue
of home, the lighted room, warmth, someone there.
Anyone will do.

Someone We've Heard a Lot About

His point-form self, his soul
if you like, is beaded
on chains of anecdotes.
          That's one way
             to know a man, and who's to say
          it's not the best.
He sports a fine follow-the-dot
shape which preens and gloats beneath
a cut-out coat,
and his image is seeded
with metaphors set like stones in
vivid alcoholic air.

We scout
out his scrapbook skin,
the standard jaw, the optional teeth.
Rumors furnish his head with hairs,
and as for the rest
we blot it out.
          Who needs a whole
          man these days.

The Stocking Man

In the cheap chain store
the man
behind the hosiery counter stands
beneath florescent tubes
where futuristic nylon things are sold.

He is an accident in ladieswear,
bull-necked, muscle-ribbed, old,
slow shuffling, confused,
prehistoric behind the crystal cubes.

His language is effete and foreign,
(lock-stitch, fall-shade, easycare.)

He is extinct and knows it, abused
by the young-pup manager,
as hugely helpless
as a dinosaur. His hand
coarse, hairy and
speckled, spreads beneath a stocking
pleading sheerness
and something
more.

John

My young son
eating his lunch, heard a plane go
overhead, and put down his spoon
remarking, the pilot doesn't know

I'm eating an egg. He seemed shocked,
just as if he'd never known
nor suspected he was locked
in, from the beginning, alone.

Helen's Morning

Upstairs you stomp
your morning two-step; shave, wash
to a ragged whistle.

Below I navigate
my bacon and egg swamp.
The forks lie docile,
a spoon sits precious
in jam, juice brims,
plates wink pious
from a yellow cloth, toast burns.

The sink stands fresh,
already nervous
with suds; the stove waits
its turn;
the cupboards cry to begin.

A Family Cycling By

Father   leaning pre-eminent on handle
bars, his weekend legs
pump gladly, his gears
release to music,
age steams off him like heat.

Mother   surprised and upright,
one hand to her flying hair,
the other clutched
tightly, steering backwards,
where am I?

children   ride between
them hyphen-like. They pedal
harder: it is a law of physics.
Their feet
cut chromium hemispheres,
their wheels beg
speed from sunlight.
Going by
they never seem
to touch
and between them there
are no words.

Great-Grandma

Back in a melon-pink
time she learned to write
what they call a fine hand.

At eighty she wrote the same
way, tough-nibbed and Christian
she crossed all her t's
with crescent fish, drew scallops
of galloping m's, tight
little o's and cups
of c, big W birds,
sun-slit e's.

Her signature, shirred
from end to end,
a ruffle of ink
unrolling her name,
      Respectfully
           and/or lovingly,
                Catherine

Two Old Friends Who Arrived at Dawn

Driving all night
in the heated car with the radio on,
drugged by the dark and numbed by the sight
of all that air, and then –

nearly there – passing transports,
muscled and jeweled as kings,
the breath of their brakes salutes
our flashing, tires sing
and nerves jump in the dark,
cracking the sky awake, giving trees
shape and making the black grass spark
with possibility.

A Wife, Forty-Five, Remembers Love

In those days
love made us liquor
throated, made us
madhouse fluent,

we stacked up stanzas
fat enough for a feast,
puffed hymns
all day, poured
words pentecostal for
forty night at least.

And all our limbs
trailed silent
like lumber,
learning the way.

Grandma's Things

Among her things
is a generation of smooth clothes pins
in a cloth bag, some string
wound like history on a cardboard
spool, colonies of jam jars
on a shelf.

They are extensions of herself,
essential as a fish's fins,
her good rewards
as fixed as stars.

And most highly prized,
between her ice-cube trays
and Birdseye peas,
are her hailstones, now three years old.

>Like bullets they fired
>from a summer sky
>speared with cold.
>Somewhere a golfer was killed
>instantly and nearby
>a garage collapsed. Trees
>fell on the hydro lines behind
>her house.

It is required
of you that you praise
their remarkable size
though you know
there are larger stones than these.
Truthfully, they are little more than beads.

What was remarkable was the speed
of her forgiveness in the first hushed
minutes after the storm when she rushed
into the ruined yard and filled
a saucepan with hail as though
it had been a presentation of some kind.

What Our Toronto Friends Said

Having an hour to kill we drove
around town, down streets with names
like Church, Jane, Martingrove,
past rows of houses set in frames.

Squared off, hedged in lots
in multiplying rows hold
splitlevel ritz, colonials with flowerpots,
freckled with signs, deadend, sold.

A neighbourhood blistered with age brings
ruin to a doubtful core,
and pagan bungalows crouch in obedient rings
around the Dominion Store.

Further out the box with its concrete stoop
in a muddy yard, the big cheap
semis with bland bargain faces, a group
of Tudor princes phony with sleep.

Then the persistent thought
intrudes, of all the people in all the rooms
sitting in chairs with the lights turned on, caught
in temporary tombs.

It seems that houses are shells that merely
help us forget by muffling the sound
of separateness. Furthermore, we see clearly
there's not enough glory to go around.

An Old Couple Who Have Loved Each Other

After all this time, quiet connects
    them like a cord.
    Hardly a word
    is required now.

Even their thoughts are cross-indexed
    which allows
    them to communicate
    with unleavened
    brevity.

Symbols will do
    and old-age verbs
    are few –
    sit, sleep, walk
    and especially
    wait.

No need to ask when or how
    age being only
    a tenured disease
    and the gate
    to a childish heaven
    electric with talk.

A Friend of Ours Who Knits

You'll see her always through a whir
of knitting needles, obscured
by her jigging wool.
She more than keeps
time; this is her way
of swimming to safety.

Odd, or perhaps not so odd,
for in the Newtonian universe
energy is energy
and who's to say
what power is hers.

The mittens that leap
from her anxious wool annul
old injuries and rehearse
her future tense.

Her husband's career is secured
in cablestitch, and her children, double-ribbed, are
safe from disease.

knit, purl,
she goes faster and faster.
increase, decrease,
now she prevents
storms, earthquakes, world wars.

And limb by limb, row by positive row
she is reviving God.

A Physicist We Know

Even while
we talk, he abstracts
himself, making terrier
leaps of speculation
on the quiet.

His smile
is detached and social,
disenfranchised by
his secret alphabet
of air.

Occasionally
he emerges in fractions,
lopsided with camaraderie,
looking rather
hysterical
and frantic.

Then we see him sympathetically
as an exile
and don't dare
ask, is it lonely in there?

Someone We Haven't Seen in Years

We never lose
touch, not completely.

His Christmas cards arrive
faithfully; his children stare out
polite from snapshots,
flashbulb dazed, and once his wife
appeared in the background, saintly
looking and dull.

His ritual paragraph of news
lurches with lame
excuses, not really warranted,
and his phrase have got
arthritic and overly cordial.
(Ours are the same, no doubt, no doubt.)

And yet we scurry down parallel lives,
probably even use
the same toothpaste, hum identical
tunes in the shower, absorb the same
revolutions and state funerals.

Anyway, we keep one shapely memory:
He, smiling from a window, hands spread
half-Hebraic in a silent-movie
shrug, mouthing prophetically,
it turns out,
see you in the next life.

Two Little Girls Dressed as Witches

In this old town along dark streets
the children are going
pilgrimlike, house to house, begging treats
by pumpkinlight, orange-red glowing
from porches.

                Black nerves
perch on their shoulders and branches curve
with meaning, making a frame
for ceremony.

They hesitate, playing the game
of inside-out, hoping the ghost they meet
is real, fearing it is, knowing
it might be.

An East Coast Friend of Ours Writes from the West

Lying in our sleeper we pushed
    back dark air all night, to wake
to blue-green bush
    and wind like a muscle on the lake.

High in the Vistadome we
    overlooked our train, and like beings
cut loose in space could see
    the earth's indifference as if seeing

it for the first time. The spreading
    land was cold, running
away from us as though dreading
    interference while the cunning

cities popped up at night. We wired ahead
    to Winnipeg to let them know
we were passing through. Fifteen minutes we said,
    and they were there, standing in a row

on the platform, a grandmother,
    aunts, some cousins. We tumbled out
cheering and touched cold cheeks together,
    talking until the conductor's shout.

Then crying good-by we piled
    back in, and for the rest
of the way the land smiled
    warmly at us, all the way West.

A Wedding We Went to Once

The Groom:

> Before you broke
> the midnight charms,
> a click of the radio put arms
> around me, arms I needed then.
> Radiant diskjockeys spoke
> to my only disease,
> well known in radioland.
> And the thin syrup of a band
> playing, suspended
> my sickness like smoke.
> The light from the dial eased
> me as much as music and,
> for a while, was my friend.

The Bride:

Before you came
with your not quite
holy love, the dialogue
in my head
had gone on for years.
It was a game
I needed then,
played out of sight
and left unsaid,
my midnight catalogue
of questions and answers
which led,
over and over again, nowhere.

An Acquaintance of Ours Who Is an Obsessive Christian

Where the cross of water
meets
the cross of wood,
he sees
    separation and the
    beginning of grief.

We would unpleat
his sadness if we could,
but the subtle vertebra
of his belief
    is knobbed with mysteries
    too prickly to touch.

It would be too
difficult to understand.
It would take too
long and
    besides, it doesn't matter
    that much.

The Barman in Halifax

Tattoos.

You seldom see them now,
but watch the barman
rolling up his sleeves,
glistening in the beer sweat.

Those are vintage marks:
crown and anchor, bleeding heart,
classic interlacing leaves
wrapped round each wrist.
Even the hairless inners of elbows
initialed in blue.

Notice the ink, violent and penetrating,
indelibly set
one random afternoon of art.

It had to be,
had to exist.

imagine,
      a beaded door, a dark
      room, a seaport,
      the young skin tensed, waiting,
      the needle ready.

The Dean's Wife

When she poured coffee it was
with such purity that we ached
with awe,
which is not to say
we admired
her.

Her frescoed hand supported
a china cup while
cream curled
from a silver spout.

Do you take sugar?
she inquired,
measuring it out,
rarified as myrrh.

But we were comforted
because
as we turned away,
she moved her stenciled jaw,
shaping the smallest, faintest smile
in all that world.

A Friend About to Be Divorced

Now that he is diminished
to a spare singular,
we notice a temporary imbalance
half-perpendicular to death.

He spends
his mornings in unfurnished
space
and his evenings cracked
and rouged with gin

His vision is plural and tends
to be tracked
with old movie scripts.
>   There she stands in
>   a painted door-
>   way, floodlit and backed
>   by music, parting vermillion lips
>   in laughter,
>
>   the sundown of her face
>   filling the screen
>   with the popcorn breath
>   of true romance –
>   until the scene
>   before the scene before
>   The End.

A Mother We Know Who Has Many Children

Children, better to see the park
as it is, hurting with snow
in this afternoon's half-dark,
poor as such places go.

Witness
an accident of space
between old streets, as far
as we know
without a name
and needing none.
                    The swings
are down, the climbing frame
whines in dirty air.
bushes gather
soot, and beneath subconscious bark
trees declare diseases.
Weather brings
ruin, and no one's ever here.

Only your voices,
miraculous
across the snow,
define this place.

A Member of Parliament

Here you can see
politicians viewed from the top,
foreshortened on green carpet,
who wander about, whisper, pop
up and down, shout
and shuffle paper, discuss
with fire or doze
through afternoons of history.

Imagine if you can
one of those
bald heads lifted out
of its walnut horizons
and studied in silhouette.

Then
it becomes a mere man,
someone
misspelled on a list
who scarcely matters or even
exists

like one of us.

INTERSECT

Intersect continues Shields's fascination with character and celebration of the family, but extends it to consider relationships between the poet's persona and the *others* that she intersects with.[1] The opening poem, "Pioneers: Southeast Ontario," signals an extension of her community further into society and deeper into history.

The poems in *Intersect* are slightly darker than those in *Others*. Shields observes, "one does inevitably get a little darker as one gets older" (*RI* 54). Atwood notes, "There has always been a dark thread" in Shields's work. This more negative vision suggests the mystery of identity and hence the difficulty of knowing others. It also involves the difficulty of communicating and a failure to connect, as portrayed in several poems that conclude with rejection or disenchantment. The open-ended closure of poems concluding with questions or conundrums suggests increasing existential anxiety.

Shields explains, "It doesn't matter how well insulated you are, you're going to get glimpses of that chaos ... It is a kind of angst when you suddenly feel you're alone and powerless and nothing makes sense. It's the opposite of these other equally rare transcendental moments when you suddenly feel everything makes sense and you perceive the pattern in the universe ... They are what poets are always trying to write about. What Byron called 'the everlasting moment'" (*RI* 45).

NOTE

1 In his review of *Intersect*, Eric Thompson judges, "Shields' observations of the world proceed from a remarkably sensible appraisal of the persons and things which matter to her: family, ancestry, friends, and life in southern Ontario" (102).

Pioneers: Southeast Ontario

They existed.   Butter bowls
and hayrakes testify,
and ruined cabins
their grievous roofs
caved in.

But they're melting to myth,
every year harder to believe
in, and the further we travel away
the more we require
in the form of proofs.

Of course
you still meet those who
are old enough to
claim kinship, but eye
witnesses are scarce
now and unreliable.

We want sealers, cutlery, clods
of earth, flames from their fires,
footsteps, echoes, the breath
they breathed,
a sign, something to
keep faith by
before they go the way
of the older gods.

Mother

While we slept our mother
moved furniture.

Through dull unfocused
dreams we could hear
the coarse scrape
of chairs and the sharp sound
of her breath easing
the sofa in place, its plush girth
opening fresh wounds
in the wallpaper.

In the morning we found
the amazing corners, startled by pure
circuits of light we'd never
seen before, pleasing
elbows of space and new shapes
to fit into   bringing us
closer to rebirth
than we ever
came   in all those years.

Friend: After Surgery

Flowers bloom
their kindest, and nurses sprout
minor rhetoric,
but rhythm is the only way out
of this dark room.

His eyes avoid the inked blurt
on the official chart.
He's busy enough with
the diesel hum of his breath,
the electric
thunder of his heart.

Aunt Alice Recalled

Grass gags the sidewalk
    between the church
    and her place

trumpet vines
    pierce the chalk-
    white porch
    the screen door traced
    with rust

Inside   the fern-
    crushed air,
    the fainting plush of chairs
    breathing the mid-day dinner

As always she waits
    in the walls,
    filling her total space
    touching at every turn

so that nothing must
    be explained or defined

    It's all
    here

Reading in Bed

At night
lying close together
propped up by accustomed pillows
they read in a shaded slant
of yellow light.

He is intent
on his book while she browses
happily enough through magazines.

The hour narrows
that which they scarcely miss
between
them   and turning pages   their elbows
sometimes touch by accident.

They're locked into print,
paper adheres to the skin
of their sleep, and ink thins
their dreams to water
but what does it matter.

Peace like this
is an accomplishment.

Woman at a Party

A circle bursts in another
room,   a woman's voice
flutes the air with laughter.

Her pleated alto notes
pass through walls,
pierce the furniture

and like flowers fall
on our darkly-suited
selves, gathered to discuss
Belfast.
            Then
                    ice cubes rejoice
in our glasses, gin buzzes throats
contagious with happiness.

We are saved tonight, and after
the party ends we float
home,   the muted
edge of that rising laughter
leading us

Professor

When he lectured
    words fell out like fruit,
    each shapely syllable locked
    into the next,
    his lips stitched with certainty
    and even the roots
    of his tiny beard
    were crisped with context.

What we heard
    we respected,
    but the hole in his sock
    made us love him.

    (pale half-moon of skin
    that fractured
    his innocent symmetry
      changing
      everything)

Suppertime 1950

Six o'clock. This hour
encircles itself, measured
out in voices and doors,
running water and the graceless scraping
of vegetables and showers
of steps on patterned floors.

We are so easily reassured
by mere clatter
by the sweet pleasing rise
of familiar steam   shaping
what we've more or less
come to recognize
as happiness.

Margaret, Aged Four

Locked into imagery
rare as algebra and unburdened
so far by science,
she perceives life in unlikely places.

For instance
watching the rain
and the nervous race
of windshield wipers, she explains

this one
is trying to chase
that one
out of her garden.

Just as though
the distance
between life and motion
and reality
measured zero.

Service Call

His van arrived
witty as a rooster – –
he had come to repair
our troubled telephone

From the window
we watched him race
leather-haunched up
the serious pole

And there –
leaning alone
into green-wired leaves
buzzing with gossip

he phoned from an oval
of space
pure perfect numbers
we'll never know

Emily Dickinson

Minutes hide their tiny Tears
and Days weep into Aprons.
A stifled Sorrow from the Years
And Silence from the Eons.

Rough Riders

Jogging into view supersized
in wired shoulders and thighs
attached like meat, the least
of them intent on murder,

though they surprise
us by being obedient to whistles,
lining up in tidy rows
more like goodly country lads
than contract heroes.

Huddle-time and their bums rough
out lunatic lily pads
on the comic green.
                        It's here
that they play at priests
locked in holy circles
plotting death
by number
so intricate we're glad
we came after all.

Furthermore, by sitting here
we hold the seasons still.
The sun is a striped beast,
the air just sharp enough
filling the bottom of every breath
with the rasp of winter.

Accidents

Here's a list:

a scar that licks
close to the bone   compliant
part of my skin
now   seldom noticed

our cracked and broken
teacups   penitent
on shelves   earless they're taken
along on picnics

the crushed fender
injured   resists
repair but is useful
anyway as an omen

and between us surrender

Accustomed to accidents
we're no longer even
watchful

Volkswagen

At the auto show
the original Volkswagen
is on display,
spotlit, velvet-draped,
the daddy of them all,
that same crouched shape
revolving like a prehistoric skull.

Better to forget the black
era of its origin.
Think of its prim chrome lips
instead, its likeable back,
just humble enough for humans,
the friendly hips
enclosing those well meaning
wheels, so anxious to get going,
so certain they know
the way.

Sister

Curious
the way our mother's
gestures survive
in us.

When she was alive
we never noticed
but now in the dark
opening up
since her sudden
leaving, we are more aware.

A thousand miles away in
a similar kitchen
you pause
to lift a coffee cup.

And here
my smaller identical wrist
traces the same arc,
precise in mid-morning air,

linking us together,
reminding us
exactly who she was,
who we are.

After the Party: I

Calling good-by good-by
but thinking   it's easy enough
for you, opening a blind
door on the promising dark,

but for us left behind
to forage
in this insane
quiet, nothing at all remains
of this evening.

only the ringed
print of a glass, a rough
question mark
in another language
asking what for and why.

After the Party: II

Think of us, the ones who leave,
travelling from this core
of light into the bruising
cave of weather

where all at once we
are struck by, one, the shut door,
two, the sudden cold wreathed
with silence and, three, losing
with every
step what we have so carefully
put together.

Radio Announcer

His throat is a piece of sculpture
designed for ultimate resonance.
His larynx serves the pure
mid-atlantic vibration,
vowels rolling in like vitamins
cut short by the sure
german-chop of consonants

but tasteful tasteful
pitched to avoid offense,
a public masculine
without past or future.

Though it must have been half-
sized once,
a child's voice, shrill
as a whistle.
It might have been
happy, it might even
have laughed

before it vanished
forever inside the great
humming tubes of the varnished
Philco where existence
begins at the station break.

Child Learning to Talk

Almost from the start
be uttered
knotted syllables

(miniature grammars nested in his head,
phrases burgeoning,
the verbs lined up like vegetables)

and with age
found words stuck to chairs
tables doors beds
never to come apart

and never recalling or acknowledging
that brief uncluttered
and untitled space where
he once lived on air
alone before the rain of language.

A Couple Take a Sunday Drive

Driving through these old towns
We gladly surrender our youth
And dream of a daft
Old Age   which we'll spend
In a house by the river,
A house with a skin of clapboard
Gingerbread fretting its lips
Idyllic with chestnut trees.

You'll be a Main Street Loiterer
Bringing me morsels of gossip
Delicious as candy
As well as the local lord
At war with encroaching industry.

And I'll be
A Small Town Character
With a parlor
Designed for that purpose
A reader of Marcel Proust
A writer of cranky letters
A tart old dear in amber
beads, convicted of witchcraft.

And we'll live like a pair
Of old clowns,
Snug in our gothic chamber
With turrets rising about
Us like flames of imperfect truth.
Our children will be ashamed of us
But our grandchildren without a doubt
Will write us up in essays.

We'll never give way to cancer, palsy,
Deafness, arthritis, heart-disease.
The only thing that will end
It all is the killing clout
Of sanity.

Letter from a Friend

What do you mean you don't
understand me these days?
Can't you see I'm
sewn up with sadness?
Stitched through and through with grief that won't
be comforted or identified.

Damn you, you were always
one to minimize: hormones
you finally decide
as an excuse
for my bitch-madness.

Let me alone.
Something terrible inside
me has come loose.
Give me time.

William

He's fifteen now and harmless.
At night he roams the kingdom
of our back lane between
garbage cans and cars,
in love with the breath of gasoline,
his poor brain smashed in some
stone-age accident.

He sometimes runs like a featherless
hen, head thrown back, wings bent,
yelping above the screen
of permitted sound, leaping
the roof of our sleeping
house and coaxing a referendum
from the old and faithful stars.

Betty

You can hardly remember
a season ago, a century ago
when you, faithful on your knees,
placed these papery bulbs in
earth.   Dry things, colloquial
as onions, but even then
their crackling skins
rustled with knowledge.

Now with nothing of winter
left but a few
grey collars of snow
around the larger trees,
already the tulips poke through,

    showing their tutored stems, their formal
    turbaned heads, and at the edge
    of every petal
    the remembering ridge
    of origin.

Fetus

Out of absence
the snail-curved
spine has grown
another centimeter.

Darkness is more
than climate here.
It has substance
and dimension.

Its dense-walled centre
spins bone on bone
links blank tendons
to blind nerves,

and never dreams or senses
what pours
daily from the unknown
impossible eye of the sun.

Our Mother's Friends

Before
us, before our
father even,
our mother's friends
were,

their brownish photographed lives
tender in legends
floating loose between flowers
and locks of hair.

Mary Organ the county beauty
pregnant and unmarried
at twenty jumped
from the top of a player
piano to the parlor floor
where she died
poor Mary Organ

And Grace with a stump
foot and the face
of an angel, her wheelchair
a fixture
on country roads, brave Grace.

And our favourite Lily
mere fragment she survives
for one reason only
her signature
Lovingly
L – i – ly

Class in Evolution

We sit in a circle of chairs
books open on our laps, we are
doing Darwin this week, tracing his innocent
maps of order all the way
to the cloudless solution,

watching what had waited transparent
all those fumbling years
fall open like a garden flower,
step by step confusion
closed by theory.

And no clause left for accident.
Beneath his patterned stars
it is a matter of destiny
with doomed orders huddled together
as the earth's edge, their time done.

Now we are sent, the appointed ones,
bookeating swallowing species
hungering circular monster
lunching on reasons
for being here.

Couple

Eleven o'clock
news   sports   weather
then the final
checking of the doors

At this hour the curtains refuse
even moonlight
and the dark stairs
exhausted by ritual
complain through carpet

You reach for the clock
and choose
the hour of our waking while
I adjust the bright
degrees of our blanket

The sheets slide back
We move together

Singer

Three-quarters drunk, late at night
across the subway platform, waiting
for the last train home, he swayed
serenely between two friends.

Their elbows dared
him, urging him forward
three lurching steps where he paused,
composed his hands and, self-appointed,
began to sing,

astonishing the air
with a crimson baritone, brandy-sweet,
touching us, touching even
the station roof with sound.

At the end
a Caruso bow and a bright
crack of applause
before the train came hurtling in.

From there we travelled across
the city while music unwound
to our destinations.

          It stayed
with us, carrying us on toward
the glittering transfer points,
humming in the final buses
to the veins of our jointed streets,
small as needles in the moonlight,
and still singing.

Home Movies 1962

In those days even
the sky
we smiled in
was lighter than air

hardly able to
hold the thin
waving of our hands,
but it's all there

    you
    circled in sun
    shaping a question,
    and I
    moving my head less
    than a fraction
    of an inch answer
          yes

Old Friend – Long Distance

By choice
we touch through wire now,
feeling our way
down the blue
looped lies
of electricity.

What we do say
we squander
since I hardly recognize
the coastline of your voice
and you don't know how
to deal with my hesitations.

      No wonder
you don't understand me
No wonder I can't hear you.

Uncle

When he speaks
it is with the privileged
angular paragraphs
of old essays,
his phrases antique
and shapely as jewelry.

But when he laughs
he touches new territory
somewhere sad between
language and breath
just missing the edge
of what he really
means.

Helen Lighting a Fire

We watch while
a match is offered and received

and a fire starts.
She burns twigs, leaves,
the sad feet
of old shrubs, the wrists
of young trees.

Fluent
she whispers to the blue-
footed twist
of flame, transparent
as lace

and sees
logs snap joyful in two,
their tough   sudden hearts
enclosing the heat
and lighting her face
with a smile
or something like a smile.

Old Men

First to come
the disabling treachery
of language

the slow spaced notes
of speech that detach
themselves and words that freeze
up suddenly   so much for wisdom

then the surprised foliage
of age
hoarse phrases that catch
in folded throats

beg your pardon please
if you will please
excuse me allow me permit me
help me forgive me please please

Friend of a Friend

A stranger
listed in my address
book, friend of a friend,
his name a gift given
in a time of famine.

The address is useless
now, a street without a city,
but I keep his smudged
name. Why not? It is a hedge
against disaster and, who knows, he
may love me someday or lend
me money or rescue me
in a time of danger.

Also, it is not impossible
that he carries my name
too, friend of a friend,
his claim on me as final
as mine on him.

Picnic at the Lake

We are posed for a painting,
arranged under a formal
tempera sky,
our thermos and fruit
colourful on cloth, the grass
around us green as Astro-Turf.

Behind us
little boats salute
each other, gay as vaudeville
on a stippled surf
inside a polished frame.

You and I
freeze on the surface
where we are waiting

where we are waiting
under a skin of glass
to be explained

Daughter

We've seen
her pull spoons from empty air,
small scattered notes, absolute
as coinage,

the pewter sound
of her flute
carrying her further and further
away so that often we
lose sight of her
completely.

The rapid rising stairs
of her breath astonish
our house, and the hemorrhage
of silver, netted like fish,
falls on private ground
where we've never really
been.

A Couple Celebrate Their Silver Anniversary

For some time now
we've been out of focus.
What was easy between us
once is cold as calculus.

Our nerve ends
scratch, selfish as hens
but all we can do
is make new bargains.

I let
    you love me
You allow
    me to love you.
There may be
    surprises yet.

Someone We Saw

One summer evening we saw
(incredible) on a patch
of old front
lawn, a young man sitting
barechested at an ironing board.

He was typing with such
speed   his urgent
hands swatting mosquitoes
between the lines.
He never looked up, of course.

It was, well, absurd.
There must be a law
somewhere which
prohibits this kind
of thing, and what's worse,
we didn't know
a single word
of what he was writing.

Family Friend, Aged Ninety

Where did it come from
this circus crush of colour?

The room where she sits
shakes with it,
the walls breaking with staggered garlands
the carpet deranged by pattern
Even the television vibrates
with garish daytime rainbows

She would be overcome
if she didn't concentrate
instead on her plaster hands,
estranged and bare as Lent in her lap

              Bloodless
her lips blow
this dancing parlor
out of existence while her eyes turn
in to pre-selected darkness

An Actor in the Little Theatre

Last year he starred
in Death of a Salesman.
Now whitened and whiskered
he has grown heroic,
his shoulders squared
with authentic valour.
his phrases supple with intellect.

He is rehearsed
into bravery,
the colour
of his disposition
magically reversed.

The effect
is hypnotic
but our clapping hands
release to a question
     Who is he?

Family at the Cottage

The partitions are half up now,
bony structures
of two-by-fours marking
off where the rooms will be

Nothing is quite normal –
wires complicate the rafters
and the bathtub, white-sided cow
sits boastful with fittings

The children, dazed by novelty,
pass supernatural
through walls

and at night
we fall
asleep in exotic lumbered corners
almost touching but never quite

Poet

For years we
read everything he
wrote

which is why
tonight we are
diminished by
his handshake

dismembered
by the bitter
minerals of his throat

a form of treason
it will take
longer to forget than
it did to remember

Sunbathers: Canada

Sunbathers, lotus-eaters,
all day lie
oiled and glistening
in the sweet boiled eye
of the sun   listening
to fierce tenor
tunes of heat

just as though
this were the land
of paradise

but they know
better   their inner ear
is pierced by a splinter
of ice
and they can hear
through the skeptical sand
the serious heartbeat
of winter
the puritan feather-falling snow

January

OOOOOOOOooooooooo
everyone in this house is sick
everyone   all the furniture
is depressed   even the clever
armchair so recently recovered

we must we must
do something about these walls
they are so weary of it all,
the piano's unfit
and those varnished beasts gathered
in the diningroom are suicidal,
little wonder, and the carpets are chronic

only the dishwasher is really
well   the machinery
of its blue waterfalls
cheerful as ever
its pure cycles admonish us
we hate it

Boys Playing Chess

They'll grow old
    these young boys hunched intent
    over a chess board.

Already they have the gestures
    of old men, the hesitation of hands
    hooked in air over castles and pawns
    prefiguring their futures,

each forward thrust and turn
    pre-recorded.
    From here on
    all moves are planned,

and though they can't see or understand
    and would grieve to be told,
    there's nothing left to learn
    now but a fringe of refinement.

Neighbour

From across the street
we see her scissored
off by walls.
A hand quick as a lizard
takes in the milk
and once a week a sheet
weeps on the line.
That's all that's all
there is so why envy her?

Nutty old maid   spinster
crazy woman crazy woman
her silhouette balloons on silk
tassled blinds
private as a witch or a wizard
or a goddess, letting no one in,
choosing – that's the word – choosing no one.

Carolers: Ontario

Their songs are circular,
voices etched
visible in the breath
of this colder country,

colder than that scratched
land where nothing grows
but a mad flowering of myth,

colder by far than Europe with
its stoney saviours prayerful
in doorways.

All the more remarkable
that they sing
here,   lunatic in snow
under these freezing local stars,

feeling their way
back toward the exact
centre where history
and miracle intersect
announcing another beginning.

Boy Waking Up

He woke
before the yellow rim
of the sun

and by accident
the whole realm
of existence slid
into view for one
moment

stretched under eyelids
blinding and extravagant
as film

drowning him
in a single stroke

Circles

Driving home in the dark
in the blue bridal
path of snowplows

watching circles flow
from overhead arc
lights, the pattern cut.

The shape selects
me like the moon
and I perceive my
journeys rounded by
departures and arrivals.

The brain plots angles
corners edges but

survival
clings to the perfect
curve of seasons.

As for Us

Why can't we live like
    this old clock,
    sure of our polished skin,
    set in motion by a careful key,

all our knowledge coiled in
    one accomplished spring, its wound-
    up heart, its slow
    and calculated
    letting go,

our accurate hands pulled round and round
    every day completed
    every hour a victory.

COMING TO CANADA

The concept of *Others* in Shields's first collection presupposes the concept of the self, and, indeed, her third collection, *Coming to Canada*, could be titled *The Self*, for Shields expresses the concept of self brilliantly in the first few poems of that collection. She begins at the beginning, in the tradition of linear autobiography, with "Getting Born" (120),[1] and arranges her poems chronologically, like an (auto)biography. Some poems lament the death of family members. Shields affirms, "This is what interests me: the arc of a human life" ("Framing" 4)[2]. In her essay "Parties Real and Otherwise," she recalls, "I wrote most of the 'Coming to Canada' sequence – rather feverishly and with great happiness – during a three-week vacation in France. The title came first, then the autobiographical impulse took over. I meant to take it further, right into middle age, but it didn't happen."

Her complex sense of self is memorably expressed in "I/Myself," where she *others* her *self*, dividing herself into "I" and "Myself" (123), with one observing the other, suggesting the budding novelist and dramatist: "here I am," she announces, with "(theatrical even then)" included parenthetically (123)[3]. Her sense of herself as both inner and outer presages the novelist's perspective – "a moment within a moment/ a voice outside a voice" – notably in her 1993 novel, *The Stone Diaries*, where she alternates between first- and second-person narrative method.

NOTES

1 Shields noted of "Getting Born": "I swore it would never happen to me – but it has. I've reached the age when I want to look back on that strange unstirred pudding we call childhood" (Carol Shields Fonds, Accession 1994–13, File 2, LAC). Levenson calls *Coming to Canada* "an auto-biographical sequence," as "the emphasis has shifted from others, however sympathetically observed, to the self, viewed from within" (xxi).

2 Carleton University Press, which published *Coming to Canada*, placed the following advertisement in the *Globe and Mail* on 17 April 1993: "Elegant Insightful Witty are all words which have been used to describe these little gems of poems. Best known for her novels and short stories, readers will be pleased that Shields has returned to her roots in poetry, with this first volume of her poems to appear in nearly twenty years. These autobiographical poems are imbued with Shields' gift for making small moments in life stand out." The *Kingston Whig-Standard* is quoted: "There are so many wonders in this small volume. Buy it or borrow it. You'll be happy you did."

3 Shields noted about "I/Myself": "You sometimes hear people talk about their first conscious memory. Here's mine" (Carol Shields Fonds, Accession 1994–13, File 2, LAC).

Getting Born

Odd that no one knows how
    it feels to be born,
    whether it's one smooth whistling ride
    down green, ether-muffled air
    or whether the first breath burns
    in the lungs with the redness of flames

My time and place are fixed:
    at least – Chicago 1935
    in the "midst of the depression" – as folks said
    then. The hospital still stands,
    a pyramid of red bricks
    made clumsy by air shafts – only now
    there's a modern wing
    smooth as an office tower

The doctor is dead
    not only dead but erased
    "What was his name anyway? An Irish name,
    wasn't it? – began with an M."
                        There's something
    careless about this forgetting
    something dull and humiliating

Well, he died in the war
      probably   a young man with
      smooth hands, blank face
          paved over
      like a kind of cement.

The doctor is dead

      Birth is an improvised procedure
      Coming alive
      just half a ceremony
      composed of breath,
      a clutch at simple air –
impossible
      to do it well

You slipped out like a lump of butter
      my mother said
          her voice
      for once
          choked with merriment
      eyes rolled upward toward the ceiling,
      round, white, young,
          clear
                oh shame

Learning to Talk

There's power in primitive grammars
    yes   no   be quiet
attached to polished stairs
    look out   hard   hurt
and unnamed objects in a narrow room
    get out of the way

When phrases fell like hammers
    on dizzy carpet
when words stuck to chairs
    and tables   never to come apart
when language blew up a new balloon
    almost every day

I/Myself

A moment of no importance
but there I was, three
years old, swinging on the gate

thinking (theatrical even then)
here I am, three years old
swinging on the gate

There's no choice
about this. Consciousness is a bold
weed, it grows where it wants,
sees what it wants to see

What it sees is a moment within
a moment, a voice
outside a voice

saying: here I am, three
years old, swinging on the gate

Another Birth

Someone (the face is blurred)
gave me a broad blade of grass,
split it with his thumbnail and
showed me how to hold it

It had to be stretched tight,
held just so in that small
oval new-found space
between the thumbs – then

you blew hard across
the taut green blade until
a whistle, then a wail
like a brass bird
weeping   split
the blue air in
two and my life began

The Radio – 1940

Like a varnished bear grown up
it hums by the busy wall
The front (I know) is burled oak
and there's cloth where
the sound comes through

It's a darker world at the back
a village spread on a hill
where the static is hatched
and the lights burn red
and the weather hisses
and pops

The inside of my head
is like this
(I know)
all wires and waiting lights
and people
coughing and playing tricks
and the tubes just warming up

Daddy

Weekdays he rode the L
got swallowed up in
the sweet black heat
of downtown
an office somewhere

evenings
he stood still
as a dead man
on the dry front lawn
holding the garden hose
in soft padded hands

and rescued the spoiled air
with rainbows

When Grandma Died – 1942

It was hard to be sad
when Grandma died
She was old
and never said much
never: *here's a nickel to spend*
or *come sit on Granny's lap*
At the table she clawed
at her food and coughed up phlegm
and people talked behind her back

Now she was dead
in a satin coffin
wearing a black dress
with lace at the chin and smiling too –

When no one was looking I touched
her mouth – which had not
turned to dust
It was hard and cold
like pressing in the side
of a rubber ball

Later I would look at my hand
and think: a part
of me has touched dead lips.
I would grow rich with disgust
and a little awed
by my hardness of heart

I tried to pretend
it was a gesture of love but
it wasn't. It was a test,
one of the first, one of the easiest,
something I had to do

The Methodist Jesus

Little Lord Jesus was a sissy but
We liked him anyway
He was like George Washington
And never told lies – only
Much more important   we knew that.

Big Lord Jesus in the brown gown
And sandals with kids climbing on his lap –
He was nice   but you never forgot
He was going to get nailed to the cross
Right through his hands and feet.

Our heavenly Father sat at a big desk
And could see right into our hearts
Where the swear words were and the lies
And the other things, but if you really truly
Wanted something   you only had to ask.

The Holy Ghost?
It was better not
To think about
The Holy Ghost.

It was the Christ Child we liked best
He was always asleep
And had a round halo like the R.C. Jesus
And a look on his face so sweet
It made you want to cry
He was on our level so to speak
Just a little kid   only holy.

The Four Seasons

Before the War
    was a simple place
    that we couldn't get back
    to somehow

The War
    was right now
    the newsreels kept our terror
    fresh
    our cousin Arnold with
    the Purple Heart
    was in the loony bin
    Some hero, Uncle Freddy said

The Duration
    was holding your breath
    or treading water for America
    or buying bonds
    if you had the cash
    or just doing your part

After the War
>	came peace
>	*kind of like heaven*
>	Aunt Violet said
>	only with regular-type deaths
>	like pneumonia
>	or cancer or heart attacks
>	or something simple and old-fashioned
>	and blameless like falling downstairs.

Visiting Aunt Violet

Mornings she woke up early and got
dressed. First she put on the pale pink girdle
with the hose that snapped to her thighs
next, a certain cotton housedress crisp and admirable
She was straight from the Rinso ads or so we thought
(There was a pertness in her collar and in her eyes)

Hers was the buoyant mid-American creed
You can be anything you like,
she told us straight – even President!
(not that we believed this for an instant)
Sometimes when her feelings were hurt she cried
and a fearful redness damaged her Rinso look

What would you have been, given the choice?
We asked her this shortly before she died
(impudent question, considering her age)
Just what I am, just what I am, she said
trembling at the trembling in her voice
swallowed by the pinkness of her rage

Learning to Read

Grass grows on the graves of Dick Jane Sally and Spot
They were boring and middleclass and, worse,
they were stereotypes – there's nothing worse than that.

They were put to death. Spot so lively and housebroken
Dick who never picked on little kids
Solid Jane and Sunny Sally, they were taken

away. It was unhealthy to force
the children-of-America to co-relate
with healthy kids, so of course

they had to go. Now there are second rate
kids with shouting mothers and fathers, and token
yellows and blacks, and folks who are overweight

But Dick Jane Sally and Spot did
one good deed. They opened their round pink
mouths and said what had to be said:

that behind the cipher of ink
lay a permanent unlocked code
that could unmake our stubborn fears and unthink

our unthinkable lot
and make us almost as good
and brave as Dick Jane Sally and Spot

Waking and Sleeping

White net curtains printed
with light
the daily trick
of the sun   calm
and steady like money
newly minted

and in the backyard
just past the standing elms
is heard
everyday   the loud drumming
of possibility

a kind of music
collected like alms
against the coming
of the enemy night

that other realm
which again and again dissolves
in a cunning alchemy
that dyes the curtains dark
as the pelts of wolves

their shining hair, their mouths
press at the window panes, guard
the door, give nothing back
but a gleam of snagged light
faintly remembered
in the shadow of day
a tooth, an eye

Easter

Everything shone,
polish was everywhere, in the throats
of waxed lilies, on the altar rail,
on top of the roadway after the rain,
and in the eyes of our Catholic cousins
(whom we loved and feared) picking at the glazed
ham and shrieking about the end of Lent
and Our Lady who wept with happiness and –

and now – just when everything seems poised
and about to begin, the machinery fails,

always at the moment
of resurrection it fails

The cousins fall silent, the dinner goes uneaten
grey smoke rises and rolls
across the lens

leaving behind the unanswerable thought:
just what is this for? these threats
of re-enactment? these rattling kilowatts
of light shut up in the brain
preserved in their perfect bottles

their faulty brine?

Aunt Ada

Aunt Ada never went to church
Her head ached or her back
and no wonder

She had the pies to bake
and the wash and the children under
foot and not so much

as a minute to sit and ponder
how she'd earned such
blessings or how to take

the anger from her look
or thunder
from her touch.

No one remembers
Aunt Ada much,
except she stayed home sick

on Sundays, rebuked
God, did her work
and grew a little kinder

The End of the War – 1945

There was our mother
on the back porch
waving a meat fork
and crying out the words
unconditional surrender

It happened to be suppertime
when the news came purling
out of the old Philco and
setting her on fire

She forgot to take off her apron
even. It was the tired
end of a hot day and a wonder
to see her step and lurch
like a crazy woman

If only we'd taken a picture
(we said later) and kept it in a frame –
our mother   dancing across the porch
with her single flashing weapon
uniquely in hand
crying *victory, victory* and hurling
us into the future

Entry

Grandpa who died young kept
a diary of sorts which was really
just a record of the weather
or how often he was obliged
to have his roof repaired
or when his taxes went up
or the latest news of City Hall
but once, a Sunday, in the year 1925
he entered a single word: woe

It shimmers uniquely on the ruled page
so small it makes us wonder and squint
but large enough in its inky power
to unsettle his young-manly script
and throw black doubt on other
previous entries: *weather tip-top*
or *gingko on Crescent Ave.*

and even darker doubt
on us
    who seize this word
      woe – eagerly, eagerly,
    making it ours

Snow

In those days, Mrs. Riordan says
(relaxing over a cup of tea)
we had snow all winter long

Snow was different in those days
(reaching for a butter tart)
over our heads like a kind of dream

Her own father lost half his toes
(a little wouldn't hurt)
while walking home from church

yes and colder to the touch
(I wouldn't mind)
piled around the door like shaving cream

You can't imagine how it was
(well, just a crumb)
those white walls, those blinded houses

those boundless deafened days
(I mustn't, I mustn't)
that paradise

Being Happy – 1949

When Uncle Freddy said
    MODERN ART
You could hear the spit
leaving his parted teeth

and when he said
    FRANKLIN DELANO ROOSEVELT
you felt the full thrust
of his curled back lip

When he said
    SEND THE WOPS BACK HOME
you shrank from the crass
emptiness of undealt
blows and from the redness of his heated
mouth

    Well, someone said,
taking me aside,
he's not a happy man.

Happiness was not
what I'd thought –
a useful monotony
something you could trust

It was the lucky pane of glass
you carried about
in your head
It took all your cunning
just to hang on
to it

and underneath
its smooth surface waited
a raging cavity
with no way out

Vision

Driving home from Uncle George's funeral
Aunt Marg saw his face glide white
across the highway, then rise
with a look of sorrow into the trees
– this in a family unvisited by visions.

It was bad enough, everyone said,
that she saw poor Uncle George
(a red-faced man who swore a lot)
but did she have to say so –
and out loud – and so soon after?

Just before he melted into space
he gave Aunt Marg a cloudy wink, softer
than his regular wink but large
enough to say that being dead
was lonely as hell.

Then becoming the kind of legend that
    takes root in awkward families,
        hauled out on spoiled occasions,
bringing ease or almost-ease
    stretched tight between disgrace
        and unsprung laughter

Dog Days

Dog days, our mother called them
wiping at her damp thighs and staying
in all day with just her slip
on and her nylons rolled round her ankles.

First thing in the morning she was up
shutting the windows, pulling down the blinds
so that the rooms grew dark amber in colour,
filling up with motionless air spiked
by the clink of the ice water bottle
and the whap of her newspaper seeking out flies –
– that same hand so helpless and ineffectual
in temperate times –

All day long she conspired and battled
bringing to satisfaction her dimmed corners,
folding and unfolding them carefully like
a kind of theatre, her face a ticking clock
moving forward, ever forward, to the tidal
hour, seven, seven-thirty, when the windows
could be opened, propped up, and the house unsettled
by the busyness of swivel fans and cross
drafts, working through the short, soft night,
banking coolness enough for another day,
righteousness for another season

Away from Home – 1954

The hedges had a leggy look but
the sharp leaves sprang out
greener than those at home

There was something odd about
the light, the way the sun came
up and the way it sank down

People were kinder or not
as kind, making you feel at
home or looking the other way

and coins in your pocket clinked
with a harder sound
but were quickly spent

and you started to think
that what you used to
think might be true

that
everything was different
and the same

Love – Age 20

There's something extravagant
about this   something that says
this illness is temporary
and likely to be cured
at any moment

Metaphors fall too fast
for health   scenery bleeds mad music
and the landscape tilts and sways
with the simple sayings of
men and women

and mostly
we're kinder than we thought
possible   breathing please
and thank you like children
who are bewitched
and taking turns and worrying that
this is going to be costly
in the end

But in the end
    in the slow unfolded history
    of our own green
    earth   winking with capsized
    promise and spilt panic –
    this was the only
    thing that would last

    an unearned gift of
    love   which we have
    not trusted or deserved
    or sufficiently praised

    but which
    despite ourselves
    has endured

Gifts

First there was elderly Uncle George pressing nickels
                                in our hands
and pointing across the street to the candy store
which left us grateful but uncertain about the shock of
this conversion – coinage into candy – with
no thought of saving or what money was for –
nothing but a stripped and heedless spending

Then there was a young man running in
a crowded street (which could be anywhere). His fine
face was alight with secrecy and he held aloft
a bunch of yellow flowers and as he ran
people stepped aside – willingly – to let him
pass, since what he carried was most certainly a gift

I think: what we could do with three days of
fine weather, how we would hold nothing
back, using it all, every hour on love
beginning with that primal gesture – an open hand that
bears an offering, a gift held briefly (as gifts are)
half in one hand, half in another

Coming to Canada – Age Twenty-Two

The postcard said: COME BACK SOON
There was a mountain, a faded lake
with a waterfall and a brown
sun setting in a tan sky

Aunt Violet's Canadian honeymoon
1932   It was swell and she
always meant to go back
but her life got in the way

It was cool and quiet there
with a king and queen
and people drinking tea
and being polite and clean
snow coming down
everywhere

    It took years to happen:
    for the lake to fill up with snow
    for the mountain to disappear
    for the sun to go down

    and years before COME
    BACK SOON changed to
    here and now and home
    the place I came to
    the place I was from

New Poems
(from *Coming to Canada*)

THE THIRTY-THREE "New Poems" in *Coming to Canada* (1992) reflect Shields's interest in others, relationships, and the self, as expressed in *Others*, *Intersect*, and *Coming to Canada*, while pointing in new directions.[1] That ten of thirty-three "New Poems" are from Shields's archived "Time Line" sequence contributes to the poems' focus on the past, including the seasons, aging, and death. Shields's assertion in "Confession" (158), "time's tenanted chronicle/ fills me full" (158), could provide the epigraph to this collection, as remembrance of times past predominates. Russell Smith calls the poems "radiant reminiscences" that "sparkle with insistent currency." This obsession with the past is reinforced by poems featuring clocks.[2] The penultimate poem, "Walkers," originally titled "Time Line," could be the title poem, as sea shells, souvenirs of holidays, evoke "the unnamed seasons/ of else and other and there" (190). The final poem, "Season's Greetings," celebrating Christmases past (191), provides an appropriate conclusion. Shields observes, "Our memory, however distorted, is a truth in a way. The real facts don't mean anything. What you carry away with you is the reality."[3]

The rather ominous tone of these "New Poems" is symbolized by the image of "a crippled insect" that reminds the speaker of "its power to hurt/ or be hurt" in "Whenever" (160), suggesting that all is not harmonious.[4] This negative attitude suggests a feminist perspective in "Voices," which concludes with a vivid image suggesting repressed rage:

a Chinese lady's shoe
screaming
in a glass case. (161)

NOTES

1. Christopher Levenson wrote to me on 2 January 2021: "I think that, as far as I can recall, the selection [of poems for 'New Poems'] was entirely mine, but I could be wrong about this. I have not retained any of my letters to or from Carol, but whatever I had is probably in McMaster University's archives: in my first Accrual, 1969–1994, Box 3, File S 19, there are two letters from 1990–1991 which may be relevant."
2. In "The Square Root of a Clock Tick: Time and Timing in Carol Shields's Poetry and Prose," Anne and Joseph Giardini speculate about whether Don Shields's collection of clocks influenced Carol's work: "Was her work affected when each passing moment ... was so crisply demarked? ... It cannot be a coincidence that in Carol Shields's poetry we see repeated attention to time and temporality ... Time is a recurring motif in Carol Shields's poems as well as in her stories and novels" (21–2).
3. Shields is quoted in an article in the *Toronto Star*, but the clipping in the Carol Shields Archives is undated.
4. Rayner observes that Shields's "New Poems" feature a voice that is "both harsher and more elegant, but no more personal or confessional" (198).

Sunday Painter

He comes early as an office worker, expectant
    but calm, unpacking precious pigment
    in the open air, an easel built
    like a crippled water bird, brushes, solvent
    and the self-forgetfulness that marks a dying breed,

but not quite, not quite; once he was told
    by a curious onlooker peering over his broad
    busy back that he was "good at clouds," and felt
    a spasm of joy or redemption or the blunt
    happiness of a man whose secret is at last revealed

and who afterwards is willing, endlessly, to invent
    on blank sky tinted blobs of cirrus and cumulus, pulled
    into white puffiness like wide-skirted brides
    walking through seasons, changes of government,
    conditions of health and family history,

and who, in the final few minutes of nearly spent
    light, busies himself with a quickly filled-
    in blue. "Cobalt," he announces to the clerestory
    of the closing day, his good sense briskly nailed
    down by that single word *cobalt* —

cobalt being the place where
    he lives, its blue stare
    and clarity his home address
    and refuge from nimbus glory,
      from imagination's uneasy shapelessness

Sleeping

Children resist sleep
sensing its treachery
its false cycle

noticing how the elderly
relish their sleep

putting their old bones down
and pleasuring themselves
with their gassy lungs

They don't seem
to care where they happen to be
that they're not alone
or that their mouths sag open

or how they must creep
down the long cold slope
toward a familiar well-lit dream
that puffs and dissolves
into something as simple
as the next meal
or the pleasure of falling asleep
again

Accident

Curious journeys can be imagined
 paper clips traveling inside a pocket
or burrs stuck to a sleeve
encircling the earth

If this is true
then why can't we believe
in the weight and worth
of accident or that

the best of what we know
 is randomly given
carried easily on difficult journeys
and lightly worn

Believe Me

Believe me, there is no connection
between that man in the bus
station screaming in a foreign
language and the woman
sprawled on the roadway
crushed by a car

Most injuries are
separately born, believe me,
as accidental as that little star
we happen to notice
and then can't find again

Confession

An anxious twitch of the nerves
    is all I get
    from sunsets, meadows, birds
    and all that

Mountains go flat
    on me and trees fall

but time's tenanted chronicle
    fills me full

Remembering

You are remembering a drenching rain
    that fell last spring on the front lawn,
drumming the porch steps clean
    and scouring out the sad middle
of an afternoon

It was Sunday, a day made simple
    and slow by old routines
late rising, newspapers, heavy meals,
    hours sagging with their own dead weight,
that massed blue gloom of other Sundays
    and nothing to celebrate

until that sudden seizure
    of weather, one brimming half-hour
of beaten air
    and afterwards a glaze
of sunlight brighter than
    you could bear

Whenever

Whenever I look up
from my coffee or work
or whatever   it's sitting there

this crouching half-formed thing
like a crippled insect
scuttling in its legless way
at the edge of my eye
or coffee cup

its edges are sharp
reminding me
of its power to hurt
or be hurt

while sitting there
doing nothing

Voices

At the museum certain
    objects
acquire a voice

the round porcelain
    humming, for instance,
of a Greek vase

or a Chinese lady's shoe
    screaming
in a glass case

Journey

At Uncle Harvey's grave we can't stop grinning. The old
goat, we mutter affectionately, though God knows
why. He had a face bruised and broken with drink,
a missing leg and washed-up liver, and little else.

Beside him is Auntie Mae who liked to swank,
her rouge and nylons and dabs of cheap cologne.
Once she tapped his wrist and said, "Enough,"
at which he turned and punched her powdered nose.

Something about him larger and more vivid
keeps us freshly fond, the old bastard.
Something about her, unfocussed and ashamed,
reminds us why we came and what we are.

Relics

Auntie Ruthie's fruited hat,
boat of truth
in a sea of right

Uncle Stanley's bamboo cane,
thin little wand
in a forest of fright

bodily relics burning alike
blackened holes
in a field of night

losing their shape
their name
their bite,

dying
particles
of light

Fortune

Our bad cousin could do
card tricks and headstands

He flunked St. Vincent's or got
thrown out we never knew

and married badly a girl
with crossed eyes who

died leaving him a dirty house
and four little kids,

the oldest who grew up to be
a doctor of divinity

and the second, a nurse
with the International Red Cross

and the next oldest, the mayor of a
medium-sized city

and the youngest, a tarot card reader
well known in the vicinity

and patronized by middle and upper-income clients
who swear by her astounding acuity

her starry predictions, her lucky guess
work, her steady gaze

her bare white arm stretched forward
fortune burning on every finger

Aunt Violet's Things

Out of a book falls
a fluttery paper shape
1943 – pledging eternal
love, bordered with lace
sealed with symmetry
and on the back, sweet
sweet blandishments

Niggling parody
of that truer heart
infinitely more fragile
shy, misshapen and spent,
beating in its own rough cage
merely to keep time

The Invention of Clocks

First imagine history as a long dull night,
a drift of unlayered absence,
impacted, unknowable, profound until
that moment, a Sunday? (1274 some say,
guessing of course) when a young man
(probably) a sword-maker by trade
(here picture him as he may have been,
smallish and thoughtful and wearing
a coarse shirt and suffering – who knows –
from medieval angst, certainly boredom)
playing idly with an iron toy newly made
a thing of teased springs and wheels
and weights, queer marrying of metal parts
mathematics and foolishness – all
this so that whatever it is, that substance
that stands between the lifting and lowering
of his wife's hand (she is dropping turnips
into boiling water) can be measured
defined, possessed and offered back
to God who swings his musical old beard
like a pendulum

At the Clock Museum

Something kingly
    in the quality brass, smoothed
    wood and quiet pedestal suggests
    a race of royal furniture
    dwarfish with faces and ticking throats

and fitted doll –
    neat doors   hinged and modest
    hiding nested springs, fine-toothed
    wheels, escapement, pendulum,
    weights, and always always a cheerful
    oily willingness to "keep" time

or at the very least to measure
    and record that insoluble
    other-water in which we float
    or sometimes   but rarely
        swim

Now

Sunday night
moon chip

pollen   grit   ash   mote
grain of sand
speck of salt

seed and crumb
drum beat

silt from pocket
comma   dot
fear of nothing   kilowatt

tick tock   paint drop
dry like an atom
hard as thought

shock to the hand
catch in the throat
mid   night
day   break

Quartz

Quartz counts the hours now
so accurate, clean and quiet
that old Ma Greenwich could fall
down dead and never be missed

But cool moonly rituals
oddly persist,
their ironic minuet
of advancement and retreat
giving sly pleasure

and the words too –
equinox, solstice

Calendar Notes

FLY PAN AM
the calendar trumpets

holidays circle
blink and bow

leap year squints
feints and conjures

mon thru sat
obedient children

sunday anarchy
violent red

twelve paper moons
ready to roll

Getting

Getting
older we take
chances
with this useful love.

Like skaters turning
and pirouetting
on a winter lake
seen at a distance,

    we've been learning
    the double trick of balance
    and indifference

Caragana

That freak current of air reported on the news last week
was only spring approaching the western suburbs

First the parkland, then that long strip south
of the boulevard, then the chill rectangular yards

of brownish bungalows. Out of nothing, out
of knitted air, the caragana has sprung

to life, its leaves doubled and tripled
during the course of one thick muffled night

dreaming moisture from the moon, remembering sun
imagining tender lattices of light

establishing its tough dominion, spreading
truant through the fence, presumptuous, defiant

but keeping a deceptive feathery look
leggy, seductive, feminine, like

young girls in costume
dancing, foolish and compliant

Spring

We're older this year
and as for spring we love
it less   violets, new leaves,
the tender unfolded air

mean not renewal but heaviness,
a coldness at the core,
like ourselves, honest, sober,
whom we also love less

Cold Storage

A month ago these same coats, capes, stoles
moved along cold springtime streets,
slipping into chilly cars, clutching at the last
spilled April accidents of weather

Wolverine, fox, beaver, mink
distinguished by quality and by dollars, by cut
(what's in this year, what's out),
by workmanship, size of pelt, genus,
species, family, coming down at last
to the creature itself (domestic or wild),
bones moving under fur,
blood, sensuality, a soul
some think, a brain of sorts, and instinct
which is – in the end – only a vast
unknowing, a muffled incomprehension
of itself, all split, sewn and styled
into seasons of new usefulness.

And now with stunning suddenness
they have been brought together.
Here flared exotic leopard meets
dyed rabbit: cleaned, bagged, insured, abandoned
to steep darkness, to plastic-swathed suspension.

Here machinery hums a perfect winter,
imposes hibernation from the wind and sun,
miles away from those natural/unnatural predators
lost to jointed memory, lost
under satin lining, sleeves and collars

so that the last feeble impulse is a giving
way to gravity, an unblinking absence
of that habit we call living,
a shut room, cleanliness, a season of silence.

Tenth Reunion

The evening itself dissolves

though later we regard
our photograph selves
pop-eyed with recall
mouths wild and scared
— *you're looking just the same!*

The camera brings resolve
and reason, a hard
focus on a bright wall,
the image that we came
here for, but can't afford

Daylight Saving

The year is cut and spliced
at night   it's painless that way.

A Public Act   pragmatic but sound,
since the hour lost is practically free,
costs nothing   in fact,
and fits neatly   poetically
(you might say) in the hour found,

saving you sooner or later or   never
a stroke of cancelled grief or rapture,
more lustrous than the hardest coal
and loose   as mercury.

You could build a house there
in that hour   and a garden, shining
windows   flowers,
a high tight   fence,

or help yourself to a single moment,
randomly chosen   unproven   unfelt,
but sealed in a gel so pure
and white and weatherless,
you want to take it on your tongue,
to let it burn or melt
there   leaving behind its puzzling trace
its teasing fragrance.

House

Now that the house is officially listed
we like it less. Partly it's that
we're constrained by order, by the dusted
mouldings, touched-up paintwork and the flat
white untruthfulness of patched
over plaster. This is a house tuned
now to the better buyer, pitched
for the executive trade,
for those who want a pleasing address and a treed
lot, graciousness and, well, a certain
sense of, you know, tradition –
like birthdays and singing around the
piano and Sunday dinners, et cetera –
apportioned happiness waiting in the walls or
winking lewdly, grinning ear to ear

The Class of '53 – Thirty Years Later

Behind the photographs, under
the white faces stunned by light and
blinking back the dazzling arithmetic
of privilege, there we were,
composed and serious, and waiting for
the future to be revealed

as though the future had been bought
already like a solemn object
paid for by red roses and the white
of dresses, by dark suits and sealed
documents, by the false rhetoric
of the class poem, by nostalgia's inaccurate
and heartbreaking damage

There between Korea's tiny thunder
and the else and otherness of that much darker storm,
we waited for what was solid and calculable,
a sort of stamped and dated coinage
we could count and weigh or save
or possibly spend

And never this: this scarcely breathed-upon
mirror, whose long angled surface
bends with shifting colours,
of failed innocence and acts of grace,
of our scalding graffiti hearts,
our real estate, our marketplace,
our calm revisions, our sons and daughters,
our accident of health, our false alarms,
of accomplishment, love and language
in its hundred-thousand parts,
of words spoken on a windy night
or in a sunstruck room
and ourselves, gathered at the future's edge,
who still contrive by trickery or courage
to take it in our arms.

Wedding

The bride stands in white
fullness on the church steps
while cameras catch a mixed
show of joy and bafflement,
sunshine and blinked-back surprise
at the suddenly unfurled
afternoon of sentiment

and also the blue fixed
shock of hurt in her eyes
when she looks up and sees
storms of confetti hurled
with such precision, such fury that
she must freeze and ask herself what
it means and if it ever stops

Holiday

Palm trees sudden as headaches
pop up, foolishly overlap
with leafless oaks
and poplars   bringing confusion

and we are uneasy about the sun,
loud bossy cousin
of the other sun

and can't quite cope
with the shock of our own
bare legs, so beggarly, so thin
like bony white orphans
we can't wait to abandon

Falling Back

It's easily done, spring and fall,
a dial turned or hands pushed and suddenly all
our lightly traced routines
    are differently lit—

Morning lopped
off, stone-cold and sharp with
crevasses, cutting harsh
    corners off yellow kitchens

But evenings yield,
grow soft, mouse-like, crushed
with fur, and cars
ascend greyed air
wave on wave, rising,
while children test their breath
    against emboldened light,

but cows in shadowed fields
scarcely move or lift
their heads
    and trees don't care

Seasons expand and shrink
    minutely

Planets cruise unstopped,
    their unaccompanied flight

Fall

This is the time of year when golden-agers
are taken on buses to view the autumn foliage
as though the sight and scent of yellowed trees
will stuff them with beautiful thoughts
and keep them from knowing –

as if there were still a trace of undamaged
hunger – for simple beauty, for colours,
the sun falling frail on the fret
work of every leaf, the trumpeting surprise
of the earth turning, returning.

Amazing the way they sit there oohing and ahhing,
behaving themselves and choking back their anger,
while non-stop movies play behind their eyes
scenes of unfiltered light
and focused rage –

God's handiwork, one of them piously announces –
and maybe when you get to be that age
you're willing to take the metaphors
you get, just to keep going:
dried sap, shrinkage, brittleness at the heart

or else the blind unthinking leverage
of custom, of perverse habit,
assembling around a summons to praise
what is fading, taking the corners
quietly, making the best of things

Together

Together so long
we've grown to look alike
    there's truth
    in these old myths

You speak
unrolling my own
thoughts   breathe with
half my breath

        at night we dream different
        dreams   but last night woke
        at the same instant
        as though an alarm
        had gone

Work

All afternoon we stacked
wood against the garage.
It was hard work
made harder because
you were fractious and exact,
wanting neat terraced
rows of light and dark
while I would have put them any old way.

Afterwards we drank tea
and noticed how our hands shook
clumsy as paws
with the tiny cups,
as though the shock
of moving from brutal bark
to flowered china
had been too great

Walkers

Walkers on a beach shiver
in sweaters   observe
the dull hinged sky   the flat glint
of pressed sand and vacant heavings

Then absence pulls together
the missing swimmers,
striped towels and picnic leavings and
prim sails from the summer nations

Shells crushed underfoot hint
at others carried home   rinsed
under city taps   set out on shelves
or on occasion lifted and turned
in winter hands

and praised for their calcium curves
the colour of harbours
their thin-edged forms
that hold the unnamed seasons
of else and other and there

Season's Greetings

These crisp cards coming
out of nothing but
the reckoning of calendars

rattling through the door slot
fresh from aircraft and thrumming
with miles, their indistinct
messages scratched and signed
on the silvered backs of
angels and snow
scenes
    bringing not
knowledge or good cheer or love

but an eye blinked
backward at other richer
seasons, something more slender
than truth and more kind
    or less kind
than letting go

Mary Swann's Poems in *Swann*

WHILE MOST OF SHIELDS'S POEMS are brief, those embedded in her 1987 novel *Swann* are unusually short – mainly cryptic couplets or quatrains. If her "New Poems" in *Coming to Canada* are rather negative, the majority of the verses in *Swann* are dark indeed. Shields's feminist indignation, or rage, hinted at in Reta Winters's unsent letters in *Unless*, erupts in Mary Swann's poems. Four of her poems are included in "Time Line": the pithy couplet "Ice is the final thief/ First cousin to larger grief" (140), the poem beginning "A simple tree may tell the truth," the two quatrains beginning, "Like a cup on the shelf" and "The mouth in the mirror is shut," as well as "Lost Things," the poem that concludes the novel, while the others may have been written specifically for *Swann*.

PART ONE: SARAH MALONEY

The rivers of this country
Shrink and crack and kill
And the waters of my body
Grow invisible. (*Swann* Epigraph and 73)

A simple tree may tell
The truth – but
Not until
Its root is cut.

The bitter leaf
Attacks the Stem,
Demands a brief
Delirium. (*Swann* 8)

A morning and an afternoon and
Night's queer knuckled hand
Hold me separate and whole
Stitching tight my daily soul. (*Swann* 19)

Iron flower of my hand
Cheated by captured ice and
Earth and sand. (*Swann* 25)

Into the carpeted clearing
Into the curtained light
Behind the sun's loud staring
Away from the sky's hard bite. (*Swann* 26)

Minutes hide their tiny tears
And Days weep into Aprons.
A stifled sobbing from the years
And Silence from the eons. (*Swann* 48)

Blood pronounces my name
Blisters the day with shame
Spends what little I own,
Robbing the hour, rubbing the bone. (*Swann* 57, 184)

PART TWO: MORTON JIMROY

"Alone in the House"

Pity my blood hidden and locked
Pity my mouth shut tight.
Pity my passing unlocked
Hours, pity my unwatched night. (*Swann* 117)

A green light drops from a blue sky
And waits like winter in its jar of glass
Tells a weather-rotted lie
Of stories of damage and loss. (*Swann* 131)

Ice is the final thief
First cousin to larger grief. (*Swann* 140)

PART THREE: ROSE HINDMARCH

The mouth in the mirror is shut.
Thought is eaten by thought.

The rooms in my head are bare
Thunder brushes my hair. (*Swann* 170)

The mirror on the other side
Opens the place where I hide. (*Swann* 171)

Feet on the winter floor
Bear Flowers to blackness
Making a corridor
Named helplessness (*Swann* 202)

Redness of cold, circle of light
Healing the heart when the hour is late (*Swann* 205)

———

A pound of joy weighs more
When grief had gone before (*Swann* 215)

PART FOUR: FREDERICK CRUZZI

―――――

Jewels of uncertain colour
Flowers of evasive scent
Stars of shifting distance
And hands that hesitate never (*Swann* 221)

―――――

Like a cup on the shelf
That's no longer here
Like the friend of myself
Who's drowned in the mirror
The hour is murdered, the moment is lost,
And everything counted except for the cost. (*Swann* 223)

―――――

Let me hide.
Let this kneeling-down pain
Of mine
Wait safe inside. (*Swann* 234)

What seems
A broken memory that tears
At whitened nerves
Like useless dreams
The night preserves
In sealed undreamed-
Of jars. (*Swann* 247)

Lost Things

By Mary Swann

It sometimes happens when looking for
Lost objects, a book, a picture or
A coin or spoon,
That something falls across the mind –
Not quite a shadow but what a shadow would be
In a place that lacked light.

As though the lost things have withdrawn
Into themselves, books returned
To paper or wood or thought,
Coins and spoons to simple ores,
Lusterless and without history,
Waiting out of sight

And becoming part of a larger loss
Without a name
Or definition or form
Not unlike what touches us
In moments of shame. (*Swann* n.p.)

Snow Poem Sequence

SNOW, AN UNDATED SEQUENCE of twenty-nine prose poems,[1] is composed of the correspondence between two sisters: one, not yet twenty, who has married and immigrated to the new world, presumably Canada, probably Ontario, and another who has remained, unmarried, at home in Suffolk. They inevitably suggest a fictional intertext with the literary production of the Strickland sisters, Susanna Moodie, author of *Roughing It in the Bush* (1852) and *Life in the Clearings* (1853), and her sister Catharine Parr Traill,[2] author of *The Backwoods of Canada* (1836) and *The Canadian Settlers Guide* (1855). Shields wrote an MA thesis at the University of Ottawa about Moodie, which she later published as *Susanna Moodie: Voice and Vision* in 1977. Moodie also forms the subject of the biography by Judith Gill, the narrator/protagonist of Shields's first novel, *Small Ceremonies*, in 1976. *Snow* may have been inspired by Margaret Atwood's *Journals of Susanna Moodie* (1970), which, Shields says, introduced her to Moodie, as "The Two Susanna Moodies," her archived essay for a graduate course at the University of Ottawa, confirms.

"My Dear Sister," each letter begins. Shields layers the narrative by including a young scholar, aged twenty-five, who reads the sisters' letters in the present in a reading room in London, presumably the British Library, recalling the dual narrative of John Fowles's *The French Lieutenant's Woman* (1969) and A.S. Byatt's *Possession* (1990). He imagines the sisters' letters as "the scripted tunnel into history" (13), recalling the tunnel through the snow that connects the sister and her family with their livestock.

In the twenty-ninth and final letter of the sequence, the married sister recalls picking flowers on Black Hill with her spinster sister in their youth. The image recalls Persephone picking flowers with her companions on Mount Etna – a black mountain, indeed – where she is kidnapped by Pluto, or Hades, and carried off to be his mate in the underworld – a myth Shields invokes in Norah Winters's disappearance in *Unless* (2002).[3]

NOTES

1 The typescript, each poem typed on a sheet of legal-size blank white paper, is headed "Carol Shields, 12/14 rue Xaintrailles, 75013 Paris, France." Poem number 27 is missing. Don Shields dates their residence at that address to the fall of 1986 and winter of 1987. Shields's "Snow" Poems are in Carol Shields Fonds, Accession 1994–13, Box 20, LAC. Poem 27 is missing. Verses 24 to 29 are in Carol Shields Fonds, Accession 1994–13, Box 20, File 3, LAC, labelled "Various poems."
2 Shields also noted the theme of "sibling rivalry between [Susanna Moodie] and Catherine Parr Traill, who was a little older and more beautiful" (Wachtel 39).
3 For a fuller discussion of this concept, please see my essay "'Because She's a Woman': Myth and Metafiction in Carol Shields's Last Novel, *Unless*."

I
The early settlers
wrote home about
the snow
They wrote about the snow
as though there was nothing
other on their minds,
No disappointments or failures and no
wish ever
to be anywhere else

2
My Dear Sister
(one such letter reads)
These last few weeks have
painted themselves on my imagination
as nothing else has ever done.
How I wish this pen of mine
might alter its shape and become
a water colourist's fine brush
that this foolish page
might convert some measure of the Divine
Beauty of a vast sky stirred
and made silent by millions on
millions of drifting flakes.

(She continues and continues in this vein)
My palate, Sister, would require white
most certainly, but also indigo, grey and
a tender rose. The dear cascading flakes
have scarcely stopped falling
these twelve days, and we are told
that an entire fortnight of snow,
especially in the month of February
is not unknown
Remember us in your prayers

3
Such letters as these were signed,
sealed and handed to trusted friends
or random travellers, whichever

Their contents entered forthwith
the chambers of chance, and lay
dormant if all went well
at the bottom of leather sacks
or the damp holds of ships
whispering with vermin

their rustle of language trapped
in foolscap, made private and strange,
and forgotten for weeks at a time,
more often months

4
It is summer, a morning in early June
when a letter arrived in a Suffolk village.
Sister reads it once, twice, three times, while
seated on the smooth stump near the cottage door
Around her feet butterflies trembled
and sped. She is a spinster,
aged twenty-seven, elegantly misshapen,
with one shoulder, rising
higher than the other, so that always she
seemed in the act of greeting or bidding farewell.
Her hair rises in a steep dark crown.
Two men have asked for her hand, but
she lacks the heart for it, loving
God, but shrinking from the union
blessed within His church (and the brutal intimacy,
thereby, which married women sustained)
Even the moaning and mating of common
animals caused her grief but
a thousand times worse was the thought
of her sister, her only sister, not yet
twenty and miles across the ocean
obliged to open her body and admit
the perplexity of alien flesh
She cannot imagine it,
how the act begins and ends
how it unfolds and
with what seeking gesture draws
itself to a conclusion.

It is unthinkable, as unthinkable
on this fine summer morning (the air
with its hot aroma of hay and manure)
as the description of snow that occupies
the greater part of the steady page

5
As I lift my pen
I record the twenty-third day of snow
The stunning morning surprise of snow
across the doorway. Snow rising
to the very sills of the little windows
one on each side of the door
Marbled drifts of great depth and weight
which require the digging of a tunnel
between house and barn so that
the animals might be fed and given straw
WE are all one, house and barn
beasts and beings

And in the spring we will be building
a second room (the letter concluded)
for God has blessed us
and before snow flies again
we will be three

6
The young scholar –
you can see him with his bent neck
at the far side of the reading room,
you can observe how he spends his hours
reading old letters, bundled together
like leaves and pressed tidily into numbered
folders. Their survival is an accident
the most fortunate kind of accident, but
what they yield is a sighing obedience
to form and order

His chief tool of perception, at age twenty-five,
is his ability to smirk
Only a year ago he taught himself
to despise what he had previously
enjoyed. Most of history, he thinks,
is as negligible as the air
between the cornflakes his landlady sets
before him in his south London lodgings.

He is attuned to his own ambitions
which are modest
and to the dying vibrancy of words
uttered

7
M. will be staying to help us with the harvest
and then —
The harvest has been somewhat better than expected
thanks to M.
M. has made himself so useful with the farm work
that it has been decided that he shall stay
as hired man throughout the winter
I should tell you, dear Sister, that M. is
a papist, but he can mend a shirt as well
as a woman and is not averse
to rocking the baby's cradle
when I am busy with my tasks.
Best, he provides cheerful companionship
when I would be otherwise made solemn
by long days of solitude.
The wondrous pure snow has heaped itself
once more around the walls of our little
house, and a glance through the window gives
back the dazzle of glassy embroidery.
It is like being sealed inside
a rugged sailing craft,
bravely adrift in a white sea.

8
It shames him, his need
for warmth, the way
he seeks it out, moving
from one small island
of heat to the next

The light is never
bright enough, burning
dimly in a narrow hall

cold trapped
in every corner
and darkness

9
The Suffolk winters tend to darkness too
and to wind and rain – and scarcely ever snow.

But in the month of December, just days
before Christmas, there was a gentle sifting down
like wetted sugar, later on an afternoon,
that left the top of the Black Hill
behind the village mantled with frost,
and around the roots of trees
there appeared pale sloped ovals of white.
The very air rang with thrilling echoes!

(these words written by Sister
in a letter which has not survived)

10
Once a month he writes home –
Canada, Winnipeg, his father
with his clean neck, his mother
tuning the radio, pulling out a chair,
opening an envelope with a table knife.

At a certain distance
the imagination buckles
Nothing will ever close this distance
(he declares), rejecting intimacy but
offering up a progress report
– everything goes well –
some mention of health, the cost
of living, the weather of course, cold
but no snow yet
Cheers!

II
For the present (she writes)
all able-bodied men of the region
have been called to serve.
The child and I would be quite
alone were it not for M.
whose lameness keeps him here
to carry on more or less
the work of the farm

WE have had much snow already
this winter and the trees
are dressed in gowns of silk,
the hems are wide with lace,
God's handiwork.
It is impossible to
wander more than
a few yards from home
But in the evenings
ofttimes
M. takes up his flute
and charms us into merriment

12

Sister shivers beneath a quilt, almost asleep.
Tonight she says her prayers in bed
which is only reasonable.
She prays first for her dead parents,
may they find peace in Paradise,
may they find perpetual rest
and may they (she does not incorporate
the final prayer in words, but merely blows
an image into the matted wool of the bedcover)
may they daily sink their gums into white bread
bread that is endlessly in supply
and as endlessly fragrant.

Her prayers flow into a kind of picture:
the home in the forest, the baby asleep
in his cradle and the wonder of his displacement,
how inside the delicate bones of his head he
is unconscious of geography, of the constellations
and continents and the wild air that feeds him.

She prays that her sister's bloodways have been cleansed,
that her fragile woman's opening has healed.

Finally she offers practical, patriotic prayers
for the regiment,
for victory
for signs of prosperity

13
You have to admire him a little,
still there after a long day, thirsty
for a glass of beer, sneering
at his thirst, yearning with his sharp-cornered
young man's fingers for a squat, brown glass
wetting a ring on a pub table
(so far beer is the only thing
he loves about this lost empire)

He's tempted to make a pencil slash
across the page (all this gentility,
it sets his teeth on edge) or perhaps
tear the edge of the paper
a fraction of an inch,
quietly, moistening it with colonial spit,
leaving a mark

But a churning vision of punishment
dissuades him, coward
He yawns, drifts in and out of the
swaying present, turning to another letter,
the scripted tunnel into history

14
Provisions are meagre but we
are grateful for such nourishment
as exists, though it is mostly
potatoes, cornmeal and a coarse
grain boiled to make porridge

Many people eat such creatures
as squirrel and think little of it.

Wednesday week M. killed a deer,
having tracked her for an hour
in the forest. We have learned
to read the tracks of animals
in the snow. There is news
that the rebellion has been put down

15
Sister prays, sews, visits the sick
and writes long letters (of which not
one survives) She feels the cold,
she notes the small betrayals of her body,
her undergarments dry by a coal fire

Her sister's leaving has deprived her of
certain realities that she cannot name

It seems to her that her letters
never leave her writing table,
but remain there, forming a nest
of disquietude for those that come
later, one image gleaming up
through all the others

16
His slender fellowship keeps
his neck bent as the afternoon
shifts toward evening, five o'clock.

He imagines minor rewards
and honours, a virtuously minimal
monograph titled A PRIVATE PERSPECTIVE
and a succession of beautiful women
slipping their arms through his

He writes home about cultural advantage,
the public transit system, parks.
He has moved his lodging twice
seeking warmth
He is moved to sign his letter
"your loving son" but he never does

17
Insofar as she is able, Sister
loves her young nephews
She writes them little encouragements,
works hard at words of caution
and counsel, advises them
to be a help to their mother
and father, to be cheerful and brave
and to suffer small pains without complaint
As God's children we must love what we are given and not wish for
more
(She smiles over her own sternness,
grasps the pen firmly and observes
the melody of her hand moving)

18
God has blessed us once again
with another child, this time a
dear little girl, born with
some difficulty while a blizzard raged
There has been much sickness,
fever and fits, also a scarcity of fresh meat
Even the snow has been meagre this
year. With great sorrow we bade
farewell to M. who has taken it
into his head to go westward where
land is plentiful and cheap and
the winters mild. Pray for us, Sister
and keep us in your heart

19
Taken day by day the winter
is as long today as it ever was
The ocean is as wide, every
mile of it and waves rise
and fall in the same manner.
(He thinks about this, idling over
his notes, yearning for a great idea,
longing, though he doesn't know it
for a passion of his own. Even
the ache of farewell excites him)

20
In Sister's dream
the trees are rearranged
She has been walking for some days
not in any wood she knows
but blindly through a forest.
There is a blizzard, her feet are cold,
freezing, and what draws her forward
is the embrace of a warm house,
smoke from its chimney, a thick
door through which can be heard
the sounds of music, merriment.

She wakes abruptly to a composition that
includes a bowl of apples, a pail of water,
the morning sun, some bundled wool
on an old dresser, begging to be knit
into blankets and sent away.

The word blizzard is much on her tongue
though she doesn't speak it
Its syllables are curious
and provide in the region of her
breast a sharp stitch of joy

In the village she is greatly loved.

21
It is like reading a new language
The researcher takes in the sturdy confidence
behind each shaded word,
gives full interpretation to
the slant of artifice
and makes allowance for the metaphor
of snow

The whole of the nineteenth century
(he says aloud one day
cutting across Russell Square,
kicking a wine bottle out of the way)
is buried in snow

He often thinks of home
remembering home
but never sure
just what he is remembering

22
We are numb with disbelief

The fever lasted but three
days and during that time he spoke
only twice, once to utter my name in love
and finally with great piety the name
of our Creator whose ways
are beyond all understanding,
my dear life's mate

23
Sister, pulling at a kerchief, grieves
at the punishment of paper and ink, that
sad waste of punctuation, and pity
that so little is laid bare

Impossible to speak over
this wide a distance,
to order comfort

Comfort in England comes freely
from the doorways of churches
domestic and sweet
the odour of apple blossoms
its own clean jelly. Then
the altar prepared for
thanksgiving

24
Exhaustion, the researcher has found, concentrates
itself at the back of his head
small as an acorn
Ardour can be held like a coin
in the hand
restlessness channelled into
a hour's work
grief focused into a point
of lights
a yellow candle
on a rough table plank

He imagines it all
absorbs it, how it takes
as its due a share
in the earth's history

25
We are greatly indebted to the
kindness of friends
without whose assistance
we would not have survived
this long winter
M. has returned from
the west and helps with
the animals

26
In the village Sister
is known for her skill
with herbs, her gift for healing
She has never stood by a glass
and beheld her naked self, not once,
but her body has spoken
in dreams

It would not do to wed a papist
(she writes) not to remarry in haste
but if Our Father in Heaven prepares
a new design
we must look upon it, each of us,
and give thanks

28
Indians measure time in terms of summer
three summers have passed
and so forth (the researcher knows this)

Sometimes too they fix time
in terms of the Great Snow
Before the Great Snow or
After the Great Snow

All times slides forward
or backward
from this point
Otherwise there would be
no sense of order

29
The snow this winter is bountiful
and from the window we observe
its crystalline perfection.
Its thick covering hides the woodpile
and barn in such a way
that I am reminded
of the dear Black Hill
behind the village
its beckoning shape
like a beast sleeping
how we used to go there
as children to gather flowers

"Time Line" Poem Sequence

SHIELDS'S ARCHIVED SEQUENCE of poems titled "Time Line"[1] was the source of many of the poems included in the section titled "New Poems" in *Coming to Canada*. Several poems were not included by editor Christopher Levenson, although they are quite successful. These previously unpublished poems are the only selections from that manuscript that are included in this collection.

NOTE

1 "Time Line" is a poem sequence in Carol Shields Fonds, Accession 1994–13, Box 20, Files 1–4. The poems titled "England," "Snapshot," "Expatriate," "Cliché," and "The Fall" are in Carol Shields Fonds, Accession 1994–13, Box 23, File 4, LAC.

Others

It's she who showed me the spot
on the wall   made hot
by the water pipe
warm to the hand   always there
sister/protector

It's he   brother/inventor
who tells me to squeeze my eyes
shut, and find whirlpools, ribbons,
the rippling surprise
of permanent treasure
      proudly, secretly given

Laughter – Aged 16

From our open
mouths came prolonged
and necessary laughter
that savage
half-language
of the half-young

ripe with outrageous
vowels, but softer
than any words, never again
as helpless
or as strong

Sunday Outing

We start with the penguins and find
aggressively lettered DO NOT FEED

The bears next, lazy old loafers
Sunlight coats their terrible hair

At the elephant house you hold
my hand, beast of eastern mystery

At snakes we separate
I take in fish while you writhe and wonder

And meet again by monkeys
making primordial jokes

Then admire arm-in-arm
the glide of swans

side by side
eyes straight ahead

homeward bound or
outward – who can tell

All Day Long

All day long we lived inside our skin
Water and air and skin were enough today
Not for months have our bodies shared so much
We didn't share our thoughts, we didn't think
to phone or read or do our chores
We scorned our chores today, today
we lived on air and skin and water
and stayed inside our bodies
all day long

Snapshot: Your Face

Your face
a failed snapshot
bludgeoned with sun
eclipsed by a thumb
or a blundering lens.

Erased
like an opaque question
or the smokey sum
of what was not
and what has been

Blame

Blame
married by virtue
of rhyme to
that other word

    what you give
    me and I you
        casually
        like dealt-out cards
    your honouring hope
    my tenuous core

    what you wear
    what I live
        what we tenderly
        carefully reshape
        into hands of shame

At the Cottage

Think
of sleeping at the cottage
where nights press toward
wholeness   the heft
of black   perfect sleep
where each breath sinks
a thousand yards
deep   connects
underground air to dreams cut
simple as posts

where flesh widens to walls
reaches through frozen
miles to where soft
earth-furred animals
lie tunneled in sleep

where we never
stay long   a week at most

then duty calls
us back   to imperfect
sleep city sleep   edged
with consciousness
halved by fear

but where we
are
nevertheless
closer to what
we have chosen
to be

England

In this other country
Saturday shoppers drink tea
in the literal climate
    of real cafes

knowing nothing
of the recent time-zones we
have pierced or the blue atlantic air
we have suddenly
    dropped from.

And though they clearly
exist, we cannot for a minute
conceive their multiple and random
lives, cannot believe their meetings,
weddings, couplings, nor separate
them from the buff simplicity
    of shopping bags and tea

    and the privilege
    unrivalled edge
    of having been here
    yesterday

Expatriate

From here home is reduced
to pure geography
no houses porches yards –
only a diagram of global
lines, a fissured
continent, fields, coast
bush hill lake stone
a cawl of pressing ice,
towns strung out on fable wire
and cities squared
with impossible density.

From here we can count
only the miniature
theatre of provincial elections,
prime-ministerial gesture,
the odd coin, a post
mark, a credit card,
a growing unmeasured
distance, the blurred vision
of a country lost,
the price
to be paid on account.

Somebody

Dear
sir/madam
cherished subscriber
beloved occupant,
loyal member,
honourable viewer beer drinker
churchgoer front
row centre
level three
we'll make a human
being out of you
if it kills you
nobody
is a nobody
here.

Getting to Know

We're getting to know the aunts and uncles, their humps and rumps
    and flapdoodle fuss
Their creaky music of cackle and cough, their mutter and rumble of
    pipe organ farts
Theirs stomachs, their kidneys, their rubbery gums, the sag and drag
    of their blubbery feet
We're about to join the aunts and the uncles, it's our turn now to
    bubble and gas
To gurgle and gargle and hawk up phlegm and hope that the sight
    is pleasing to them
And that nieces and nephews will look sideways at us, and not understand what we never guessed

Cliché

Poor swindled fossil moon
    run ragged by weather
    your smooth sides wrecked
    by messages
    and songs

and now your lovely crust cut
    into beef steaks
    analyzed and dispersed
    to international fairs

so that what you are
or were has burst,
shut
up in blown
out images

it didn't take
all that long

The Fall

Like a school bell, like an early hour
alarm, the first frost brings thousands
hurrying into the countryside, suddenly
and briefly made beautiful,

walkers, families in cars, buses full
of children and Golden-Age excursions
who gawk, angle, wrestle for views
and prepare to be moved by the power
of the dying trees whose
branches break through the reckless
lovely abandonment of leaves:

Here is something they can all respond
to, though it's not for the leaves they come
but to escape the pain of separateness,

to declare their shared custody,
joining in the random impromptu choirs
and laying on the hills wreathes
or witness –

lovely   beautiful   marvellous
have you ever   ever   in all your
life seen such colour such colour
such   glorious   colour

Likeness

Certain forces resist metaphor,
    gravity or the sun's
    extracted weather

but our little homemade weeks
    and days have fed
    and fattened on likeness

especially Sunday
    waiting like a cooled
    star to gather
    us in

or a steady ticking clock
    stuck in a gilded belly

or the small tufted feather
    an uncle might wear in his hat
    sparrow-soft, inconsequential
    necessary

Coping

They knew a thing
or two, those old guys.
Hairshirts were better
and thunderbolts.

The plucking out of eyes,
the rub of salt
cut through the clutter
of lively sin.

We'd rather die
saying – it's my fault
    it's my fault

        omission and commission
        observed on a platter,
        the unnerving lie
        of immovable guilt

Being Sad 1949

Sadness is an art easily learned
Its positions and various
humours   are part
of an act we like to put on
to amuse our less spoiled selves

and burn the sweet tumours
out of our brains and confuse
our buoyant beginnings and
drive the wolves away from belief
and strengthen our hearts with misgiving

The Sunday Poems

SHIELDS'S ARCHIVED POETRY sequence titled the "Sunday Poems" was the source of many of the poems included in the section titled "New Poems" in *Coming to Canada*. Two untitled poems were not included by editor Christopher Levenson, although they are quite successful poems.

Beside me on the plane
a girl in a loose wool sweater
a young man with hairy arms

He says to her, whispers, *come on.*
She says, teasing, *not here.*
I shut my eyes, pretend to sleep.

Why not, he says, all cunning.
Because, she says, all charm.
I stir ever so slightly.

Because of her, she says.
He says, softly, *Screw her.*
I open my powerful eyes, smile hard

and at once enter the furred
region of love, just me, a knitted sleeve
a pair of hairy arms.

Some people, doing the cathedrals,
of Europe, romantically light candles
to that emptying glass, their life

Others stay home
reverently watching the midnight movie
their whole lives a foreign film

Other

Discussing the subject of happiness,
A Russian friend told how his father
was imprisoned for six years
without any charges being laid.

While in prison he was happy.
He woke at five knowing
that at six he would be given
a square of bread
That made him happy.

Later in the morning
names were called out,
the names of those men
who were to go to work in the quarry

At the quarry these men
were commanded not to work
but to hurl themselves to their death.

Day after day passed and
his name was not called.
Each time his name was not called
he was made happy.

On Sundays his happiness became perfect.
On Sundays a primate edict declared
that no one was called to the quarry,
and with the squares of bread, a kind
of coffee was brought, steaming in a pail

Lifting the pail to his mouth
he thought how he was condemned
after all,
that any minute he would go
crazy with happiness

Shock

At
the end of Blue Church Road
stands a flat
and flattening truth

a respite
for moderns and half-spent cynics
a break in the broken code
of belief at
the end of Blue
Church Road where you
find: no toll booth
no tastee-freeze no manic
motor court no gee-whiz
historical site

but the unsought end
of a search
a mundane
marvel trite
and true
guaranteed to send
you soberly sane
at the end of Blue Church Road is
a blue church
say it again
A Blue Church

Inside Sunday

Inside the heart a deep
red parlor darkness

throats and shoulders
too and

roomsful of bosomy talkers,
fleeting epigrams, their small
toes showing white
and going by guesswork into

photograph albums where
ruling grandmothers are serving
sunday lunch, a loud shrewd
rhetoric booming overhead

Archived Poems

ALL THE POEMS in this section are previously unpublished and are gleaned from the Carol Shields archives at the National Library. Some poems are clearly early works, although several are undated.

Learning to Write Poems

the word is clear
and hard as a nut
more is less
or else it's not
it plays its brief tune
in this unconfessed dark
and weighs in the hand like a fork or a spoon
or bites like a tooth in the possible air
yes

Going to Work

At this hour, bus queues, cars
  blue buses nosing into curbs
Who invented these patterns, who decided to
   remove from houses occupants
    – deliver them to other rooms
       for the gathered bouquets of cash
Young girls run smooth hands down their coats
     buses nose along curbs
     the pavement receives them calmly
     trains obey, their autocratic doors cooperate
     by nine it's over
     it's all for the best

     signs flash unspeakable hamburgers
     the traffic lights perform, skillful as baton twirlers
     There is almost no talking

"we are made of stardust
a poem can alter itself into a flower, stone,
or a piece of animal scat
                      a goodly wish"

Sonnet

I guess it just depends on what you mean
By love. To Milton it was duty first,
But that was dull and dry. But if I lean
Toward Byron's fiery love my heart would burst.
And then there's Mrs. Browning. I must say
She overdid it just a bit. I will
Not take her all-consuming loving way.
Such sentiment would surely make me ill.
If none will satisfy to whom then may
I turn? Dare I trust myself? I fear
That when they ask me what love is I'll say
That feeling that you give me when you're near.
You are my definition. You alone
Can tell me what the poets have not known.

Couple

Again and again this thing
we vainly, pridefully, call
our happiness
unpins itself
a faulty brooch and badly made

a word said, or not said
or nothing at all
is enough to open
that begging gulf
between what is
and isn't, but once was

The Tea Ceremony

Spoon/cup/saucer
stand ready as theatre
and we are invited in

Sugar/milk/the arc
of poured tea
the eyelid holds it safe.

Nothing is required but
the slow dance of hands
across the table top

When it turns dark,
the light repairs itself
We may talk or not

You say that
you trust above all this cup
of charity

Which is as good a reason
as any
to hang on.

Mark Twain

I laughed my way into the hearts of men,
And finding safety there, laughed on. But when
I laughed too hard, a cynic's laugh, they closed
Their ears against my voice. And still I posed
As humor's guardian as long as I could.
Taken for a clown, misunderstood.
Is tragedy a joke? Is life a pun?
And do we chuckle over death? The sun
That lights the river's path dries up her bed
In self defense. What fools we be. The dead
At least are still. I had so much to give.
O Sophocles, did you also live
To hear the laughter of the drunken crowd?
Was every laugh a bitter cup, a shroud
Upon your great career? I have wept
The comic tears, have felt great things, was swept
By noble thoughts, inspired to create
A lasting work, a classic piece, a great
Enduring message that would move the heart
Of men who heard to something quite apart
From laughter's senseless scream. If once they would
Have wept with me, to be misunderstood
Would well be worth the shame. The writer's sin
Of having made a Huckleberry Finn
Would be diluted into space if men
Would listen to my Satan's cry. Again
I'd be repaid a thousand times if they

Would hide their laughter in their sleeves. The day
For jests is gone. O, look into my mind.
And see; I breathe, I think and yet men find
Me but a fool. Beloved, yes, but still
A fool. Must I stride the mockers' will
Forever? If there be a god, he made
A damned mistake with me. He thrust the blade
Of humour through a mind that never could
Express itself. His highness never should
Have made a jester with a mind, for I
In deep frustration know that I will die
A failure. Half of me has lived, but half
Has never been expressed. And still I laugh
My way into a grave. And on the stone
I'll carve the tragic note, at last my own.
"Laugh on you foolish men. My message tells
That heaven hath no joyous laughter bells."

Napoleon at St. Helena

When I was very young I knew a thing
That wondrous men of history's golden wing
Had never known or never even sensed.
And out of all the heavy books from whence
There poured a classic stream of precious things
That showers men with food for thought; that brings
To modern men creations of the mind,
And stretches through the separate years to bind
Philosophy to God, and God to man;
And man I am. And as mankind began
So also shall I bravely build anew
A thought unborrowed from the Greeks. No clue
I found that history was complete. So I
In pridely innocence raised up my cry
That men might hear, might hear and know that life
Was not cut off by history's classic knife.
That I would meet this challenge was my fate.
That I would be recorded with the great
Surged as a passion through my youthful veins.
O God, had I but known that power's reins
Are held by Thee, and not by earthly kings,
That what I've read in books are only things
That man has taken second hand. A sip
From heaven's cup is all we have to whip
Our dreams to passion's heat. And great they are
Who are content to find a broken star
Wrought by Thy hand; for ruined though it seems

They shall repair a world beyond men's dreams.
But heavens are not carved by mortal men.
All that is has always been, Amen.

Letters

Letters are always arriving
Dear _____ they begin astonishingly
      indicating love or perhaps not love

And at the end a scrawled man waving
goodbye-for-now or expressing sincerity
or sending all good wishes or sometimes
      but rarely nowadays promising love

a dangerous word since
generally speaking letters are read many times
over and can therefore be deceiving
bringing confusion or even injury
      when what was intended was love

It's a trick of the steadiest passion –
                    weaving
on the ready page a parody
of itself sometimes shrunken sometimes
overblown but either way leaving
behind a mere ounce
or less of love
or something like love

Holiday

Travel is the ultimate swindle,
yet here we are again,
expectant as children.

The taxi has been called
and in the hall the luggage stands
matched and mated canvas,

self-contained and locked, each
one tagged with airline flags,
destination, name, address,

announcing that this
may be the last chance
we have to deceive

ourselves with make-believe
brochure bliss, photographed sand,
a touched-up turquoise sea,

and the tide that gathers us
here in the lighted hall,
to this shallow, unlathered beach.

April in Ottawa

Behind the National Library
Beneath the rapids
Rooted to a narrow rock
A small tree
Buds.

ANNOTATIONS

Others (1972)

"Margaret at Easter":
"Margaret" is Carol Shields's daughter Meg Shields.

"Anne at the Symphony":
"Anne" is Carol Shields's eldest daughter, Anne Giardini.

"Sara":
"Sara" is Carol Shields's youngest daughter, Sara Cassidy.

"John":
"John" is Carol Shields's eldest child, John Shields.

Intersect (1974)

"Pioneers: Southeast Ontario":
Shields's draft has the note "c. 1972."

"Mother":
Carol Shields's mother, Inez Warner, did move furniture around during the night. The protagonist-narrators of Shields's first two novels, *Small Ceremonies* and *The Box Garden*, recall their mother moving furniture around at night. Shields's mother, Inez Sellgren Warner, died in 1971, the year before Shields's first book of poetry was published. *Small Ceremonies* is dedicated to her.

"Professor":
Shields's archived poem is titled "Assistant Professor."

"Margaret, Aged Four":
"Margaret" is Carol Shields's daughter Meg Shields.

"Emily Dickinson":
This poem is included in *Swann*, page 48.

"Rough Riders":
The Saskatchewan professional football team is called the Rough Riders.

"Sister":
Carol Shields's sister Barbara, known as "Babs," was a fraternal twin and was two years older than Carol.

"William":
This poem is titled "Herbie" in draft.

"Betty":
This poem was titled variously "Tulips," "To a Friend," "Woman Planting," and "Garden."

"Singer":
Shields's archived poem is titled "Toronto Singer."

"Helen Lighting a Fire":
Shields's archived draft is titled variously "Nora" and "Woman Lighting Fire." It opens with the lines:

> Primitive as a priest
> she bends to the task
> at the fireplace –

"Daughter":
The "Daughter" is Carol Shields's daughter Catherine, who played the flute.

"A Couple Celebrate Their Silver Anniversary":
Carol and Don Shields married in 1957. Their silver anniversary took place in 1982.

"Poet":
Philip Larkin, whose poetry Shields admired, may be the poet referenced here.

"Carolers: Ontario":
The table of contents lists this poem as "Carolers: Ottawa."

"As for Us":
The final poem in the collection was titled variously "Us," "The Clock Winder," and "Albert." Carol Shields's husband, Don Shields, collects clocks.

Coming to Canada (1992)

"Getting Born":
Carol Shields includes a handwritten note beneath the typescript of the poem saying, "I swore it would never happen to me. But it has. I've reached the age when I *want* to look back on that strange unstirred pudding we call childhood."

"Learning to Talk":
In the first line the word "power" replaced "a nostalgia for." Perhaps Shields preferred the alliteration provided by the word "power."

"I/Myself":
Carol Shields handwrote beneath the typescript of the poem, "You sometimes hear people talk about their first conscious memory – here's mine."

"Another Birth":
Her "life began" again when she gave voice.

"The Radio – 1940":
Carol Shields handwrote beneath the typescript of the poem, "Inanimate objects, when we're young, are, of course, alive."

"Daddy":
Shields inserted the last line, "of all things," by hand below the word "rainbows."

"When Grandma Died – 1942":
Carol Shields crossed out the last line on the typescript of the poem.

"The Methodist Jesus":
Carol Shields handwrote above the title of the poem, "and there was the other side of spiritual life."

"The Four Seasons":
Carol Shields handwrote beneath the typescript of the poem, "The four seasons of my childhood of those confused days were named:

before the war
the war
the duration and something called 'after the war.'"

"Waking and Sleeping":
Shields's archived draft ends with the words "enemy night."

"Aunt Ada":
This poem is titled "Gone" on Shields's typescript, and the opening name was not "Aunt Ada," but "Grandma."

"Entry":
This poem is titled "Grandpa" on Shields's typescript. The draft ends after the first stanza.

"Snow":
"Mrs. Riordan" is the name of a character in *A Portrait of the Artist as a Young Man* by James Joyce.

"Being Happy – 1949":
The last lines of this poem provide the opening for Shields's novel *Unless* (2001).

"Vision":
Carol Shields's typescript shows a shorter version that does not include the final stanza. The line "lonely as hell" replaces the original line: "was a goddamn blast and what the hell was not so bad after all." Shields added the lines "that same hand so helpless and ineffectual / in temperate times" and the last line, "righteousness for another season."

"Dog Days":
Carol Shields handwrote above the title of the poem, "People, looking back, distort the weather. The winters were colder and the summers were hotter. But in Chicago we always had two weeks in August when the temperature was in the high 90s." She added the last two lines of stanza two and the last line of stanza three.

"Gifts":
Carol Shields's archived draft ends with these lines: "lets it all come at you speeding / toward you with the accuracy of light," which follow the phrase "an open hand that ..."

"Coming to Canada – Age Twenty-Two":
The Carol Shields Fonds, Accession 2003–09, Box 114, File 5, LAC, contains the missing penultimate verse for the final poem, "Coming to Canada":

This love is lost in the snow
and the winter is gone
Instead of come back soon
    There is the sharpness of now.

"New Poems" (from *Coming to Canada*)

"Remembering":
The draft begins, "We exaggerate perhaps."

"Whenever":
Shields's archived draft has the line "it's always there" after the word "sharp."

"Relics":
This poem is titled "Them" in draft and contains only the first two stanzas of the published version.

"The Invention of Clocks":
The name typed on the archived draft of this poem reads "Ian McAllister," a pseudonym that Shields employed as a young poet.

"Caragana":
This poem was first published as "Winnipeg Sunday" (1) by "Ian McAllister."

"Tenth Reunion":
Archived drafts of this poem have the titles "Reunion" and "Class Reunion."

"Daylight Saving":
Shields's archived draft ends with the word "never."

"House":
Shields's archived draft reveals that the last two lines were added.

"The Class of '53 – Thirty Years Later":
The last word in the second to last line in the version published in *Coming to Canada* is "outrage," but this is probably a misprint for "courage," the word with which the line ends in the publication of Shields's poem in her school magazine (Carol Shields Fonds, Accession 1994–13, Box 67, LAC).

The last line of Shields's typescript reads, "to take the future one more time and hold it in our arms."

"Fall":
Shields's archived draft includes only the first and third stanzas, concluding with the word "rage."

"Work":
This poem was first published as "Winnipeg Sunday" (2) by "Ian McAllister."

"Walkers":
The original title of this poem was "Time." It was published under the title "Time Line." Thus, it is the title poem of Shields's "Time Line" series.

Mary Swann's Poems in *Swann*

Five of the poems in *Swann* are in "Time Line" and "Sunday Poems," including "Lost Things."

"A green light drops from a blue sky":
The poem in *Swann* has "Or stories of damage and loss" in the last line (131). "Or" may be a misprint for "Of."

"The mouth in the mirror is shut":
Shields's "Time Line" manuscript contains this quatrain, but only the final couplet is included in *Swann*.

Snow Poem Sequence

Shields's "Snow" Poems are in Carol Shields Fonds, Accession 1994–13, Box 20, LAC. Poem 27 is missing. Verses 24 to 29 are in Carol Shields Fonds, Accession 1994–13, Box 20, File 3, LAC, labelled "Various poems."

14, "Provisions are meager":
"The rebellion" is the Upper Canada Rebellion of 1837–38, led by William Lyon Mackenzie. John Moodie served in the rebellion under Mackenzie. Shields's M.A. research on Moodie would have acquainted her with this fact.

"Time Line" Poem Sequence

"Time Line" is a poem sequence in Carol Shields Fonds, Accession 1994–13, Box 20, Files 1–4, LAC. The poems titled "England," "Snapshot," "Expatriate," "Cliché," and "The Fall" are in Box 23, File 4 with the Vortex, Accession 1994–13 Q4–10224.

"Others" is titled "Sister/Brother" in draft.

"Sunday Outing":

Levenson sent me a copy of this poem, titled "Outing," along with several page proofs from *Intersect*, suggesting that it was intended to be included in that collection.

"Snapshot" has the alternate title "Your Face." The words "Erased like an" are inserted by hand.

"Blame" has the word "damaged" before "tenuous" crossed out.

"Expatriate" has the title "Abroad" crossed out, and the word "home" replaces the word "Canada." The word "voluntarily" is crossed out between the words "country" and "lost."

"Somebody" shows the phrase "just by your credit card and take our word for it" inserted before the last word.

"The Sunday Poems"

The title page says "The Sunday Poems by Carol Shields." The title page includes the following information:

Until December 18, 1985
2, rue de l'Ouche Arbelle
Boyaye, France, 44830
Telephone: 65 41 91

After December 18, 1985
701–237 Wellington Cr.
Winnipeg R3M0A1
204 284 9907

The untitled poem beginning "Beside me on the plane" is in the Carol Shields Fonds, Accession 1994–13, Box 20, File 3, LAC.

"All Day Long" is also in the "Time Line" sequence.

"Other" is titled "Condemned" in the "Time Line" sequence and is in the Carol Shields Fonds, Accession 1994–13, Box 20, File 3, LAC.

Archived Poems

"Learning to Write Poems" is a poem missing from *Coming to Canada* that was found in Carol Shields Fonds, Accession 2003–09, Box 114, File 5, LAC.

"Going to Work" is in Carol Shields Fonds, Accession 2003–09, Vol. 114, File 1, LAC.

"Sonnet":
"Sonnet," first published in *Thoughts*, the literary magazine of Hanover College, in 1957, when Shields was age twenty-two, was republished in *Early Voices*, although it is not, strictly speaking, a juvenile work, as the Juvenilia Press usually includes only works composed before the writer was twenty years of age.

"The Tea Ceremony" is in Carol Shields Fonds, Accession 2003–09, Box 92, File 27, LAC.

"Mark Twain":
"Mark Twain" was originally published in *Thoughts*, Hanover College's literary magazine, in 1957 and republished in *Early Voices*, although it is not, strictly speaking, a juvenile work.

"Napoleon at St. Helena":
"Napoleon at St. Helena" was originally published in *Thoughts*, Hanover College's literary magazine, in 1957 and republished in *Early Voices*, although, again, it is not, strictly speaking, a juvenile work.

WORKS CITED

Atwood, Margaret. "Carol Shields." In *Moving Targets: Writing with Intent, 1982–2004*, 360–3. Toronto: Anansi Press, 2004.
– "Margaret Atwood." In *A Writer's Life: The Margaret Laurence Lectures*, the Writer's Trust of Canada, 215–28. Toronto: McClelland and Stewart, 2011.
– "*Orientation*: Who Do You Think You Are?" In *Negotiating with the Dead: A Writer on Writing*, 1–28. Cambridge: Cambridge University Press, 2011.
De Roo, Harvey. "A Little Like Flying: An Interview with Carol Shields." *West Coast Review* 23, no. 3 (1989): 38–56.
Dvořák, Marta. "Carol Shields and the Poetics of the Quotidian." *Journal of the Short Story in English* 38 (Spring 2002): 2–10.
Dvořák, Marta, and Manina Jones, eds. *Carol Shields and the Extra-Ordinary*. Montreal & Kingston: McGill-Queen's University Press, 2007.
Eden, Edward, and Dee Goertz, eds. *Carol Shields, Narrative Hunger, and the Possibilities of Fiction*. Toronto, Buffalo, London: University of Toronot Press, 2003.
Gamble, Sarah. "Filling the Creative Void: Narrative Dilemmas in *Small Ceremonies*, the *Happenstance* Novels, and *Swann*." In Eden and Goertz, *Carol Shields, Narrative Hunger, and the Possibilities of Fiction*, 39–60.
Giardini, Anne. "Freight Cars, Clotheslines and a Mother's Advice." *Globe and Mail*, 24 March 2009.
Giardini, Anne, and Joseph Giardini. "The Square Root of a Clock Tick: Time and Timing in Carol Shields's Poetry and Prose." In *The Worlds of Carol Shields*, edited by David Staines, 21–34. Ottawa: University of Ottawa Press, 2014.
Giardini, Anne, and Nicholas Giardini, eds. *Startle and Illuminate: Carol Shields on Writing*. Toronto: Random House Canada, 2016.
Goertz, Dee. "Treading the Maze of Larry's Party." In Eden and Goertz, *Carol Shields, Narrative Hunger, and the Possibilities of Fiction*, 230–54.

Groening. Laura. "Still in the Kitchen: The Art of Carol Shields." *Canadian Forum* (January/February 1991): 14–17.
Gross, Terry. Interview with Carol Shields, Public Radio, 1 May 2002. https://freshairarchive.org/segments/novelist-carol-shields-0
Honigsbaum, Mark. "The *Guardian* Profile: Carol Shields, Goddess of Small Things." *Guardian*, 23 May 1998, 6–7.
Ings, Katharine Nicholson. "Illuminating the Moment: Verbal Tableaux in Carol Shields' Poetry." *Prairie Fire* 16, no. 1 (1995): 168–73.
Keith, W.J. Review of *Coming to Canada*. LMS 0212 1997–04 Vol. 51, File 6.
Lecker, Robert. "All Plot, Little Thought: Review of *Small Ceremonies*." *Essays on Canadian Writing* 5 (Fall 1976): 80–2.
Leigh, Simon. Review of *Intersect*. *Fiddlehead* 109 (Spring 1976): 130. CSF, Accession 1994–1311, Box 20, File 16, p. 5.
Levenson, Christopher. Introduction. *Coming to Canada*, i–xv. Ottawa: Carleton University Press, [1992] 1995.
– Review of *Others*. File labelled "Others" Reviews in Carol Shields Fonds, Accession 1994–13, Box 20.
Levin, Martin. "Canadian Shields." *Imperial Oil Review* (Winter 1995): 12–17.
Lively, Penelope. Introduction. *The Stone Diaries*. Toronto: Vintage Canada, 2008.
Morton, Mark. "*Coming to Canada* by Carol Shields." *Prairie Fire* 16, no. 1 (1995): 174–6.
Oliver, Michael Brian. "Scream: New Canadian Women Poets," review of *Others* (35–8). CSF, Accession 1994–1311, Box 20, File 15.
Parini, Jay. "Notable Books of the Year 1994." *New York Times* (4 December 1994), Section 7, 65.
Parpart, Lee Anne. "The Egg-Bald Baby's Cry." *Whig-Standard Magazine* 1 (13 February 1993): 17.
Ramon, Alex. *Liminal Spaces: The Double Art of Carol Shields*. Newcastle: Cambridge Scholars, 2008.
Rayner, Anne. "Postcards from Home," review of *Coming to Canada*. LMS 0212 Accession 1–1994–13, Vol. 20, File 17.
Rooke, Constance. "Carol Shields." *The Oxford Companion to Canadian Literature*, edited by William Toye, 751–2. Toronto: Oxford University Press, 1983.
Shields, Carol. Afterword to *Dropped Threads 2: More of What We Aren't Told*, edited by Marjorie May Anderson and Catherine Shields, 365–7. Toronto: Vintage Canada, 2003.
– "Arriving Late: Starting Over." In *How Stories Mean*, edited by John Metcalf and J.R. Struthers, 87–90 and 244–51. Erin: Porcupine's Quill, 1993.

- Author's Introduction. In *Early Voices*, edited by T.L. Walters and James King, 33. Edmonton: Juvenilia Press, 2001.
- *The Box Garden*. Toronto; New York: McGraw-Hill Ryerson, 1977.
- *Coming to Canada*. Edited and with an Introduction by Christopher Levenson. Ottawa: Carleton University Press, [1992] 1995.
- "Framing the Structure of a Novel." *Writer* 111, no. 7 (1998): 3–4.
- *Happenstance*. Toronto: McGraw-Hill Ryerson, 1980.
- *Larry's Party*. Toronto: Random House Canada, 1997.
- "Moment's Moment." "Chapter 1 The First Day. Monday." *Moment's Moment*, 2003. CSF, RG 11805, Accession 2003–09, Vol. 117, File 27, pp. 43–61. TS. National Library.
- "Moment's Moment: Chapter 3 The Third Day. Wednesday." CSF, RG 11805, Accession 2003–09, Vol. 117, File 27, pp. 43–61.TS. National Library.
- "Narrative Hunger and the Overflowing Cupboard." In Dee and Goertz, *Carol Shields, Narrative Hunger, and the Possibilities of Fiction*, 19–36.
- "Parties Real and Otherwise." *Victoria* (June 1998): 44–6.
- *The Republic of Love*. Toronto: Random House Canada, 1992.
- "Segue." *The Collected Stories*, 1–20. Toronto: Random House Canada, 2004.
- *Small Ceremonies*. Toronto; New York: McGraw-Hill Ryerson, 1976.
- "Sonnet." In *Early Voices*, edited by T.L. Walters and James King, 33. Edmonton: Juvenilia Press, 2001.
- *The Stone Diaries*. Toronto: Random House Canada, 1993.
- *Swann*. Toronto: Random House, Canada, 1987.
- *Unless*. Toronto: Random House Canada, 2002.
- *Various Miracles*. Toronto: Stoddart, 1985; New York: Penguin, 1989.
- "A View from the Edge of the Edge." In *Carol Shields and the Extra-Ordinary*, edited by Marta Dvořák and Manina Jones, 17–29. Montreal & Kingston: McGill-Queen's University Press, 2007.

Shields, Carol, and Blanche Howard. *A Celibate Season*. 1991. Toronto: Vintage-Random, 1998.

Skuce, Joel. "Natural, Physical Simplicity." *Canadian Forum* (November 1993): 44–5.

Smith, Russell. "Clear Eyes of a Child Illuminate Poet's Work," review of *Coming to Canada*. LMS 0212 Accession 1–1994–13, Vol. 20, File 17.

Stevens, Peter. "Poets and the Courage of the Ordinary," review of *Others*. *Globe and Mail*, 28 July 1973. LMS 0212 Accession 1–1994–13, Vol. 20, File 15.

Stovel, Nora Foster. "'Because She's a Woman': Myth and Metafiction in Carol Shields's Last Novel, *Unless*." *English Studies in Canada* 32, no. 4 (December 2006 issue; published March 2008): 51–73.

- "'Excursions into the Sublime': A Personal Reminiscence of Carol Shields." *Studies in Canadian Literature* 38, no. 1 (December 2013): 267–80.

- "'Fragments on My Apple': Carol Shields's Unfinished Novel." *Canadian Literature* 217 (Summer 2013): 186–96.
Thomas, Clara. "Reassembling Fragments: Susanna Moodie, Carol Shields and Mary Swann." In *Inside the Poem: Essays and Poems in Honour of Donald Stephens*, edited by W.H. New, 196–204. Toronto: Oxford University Press, 1992.
Thompson, Eric. "Plain and Fantasy," review of *Intersect*. *Canadian Literature* 65 (Summer 1975): 101–4. http://canlit.ca/reviews/plain_and_fantasy.
Trozzi, Adriana. *Carol Shields's Magic Wand: Turning the Ordinary into the Extraordinary*. Rome: Bulzoni Editore, 2001.
Van Herk, Aritha. "Extrapolations from *Miracles*." *Room of One's Own*, The Carol Shields Issue, 13, nos 1&2 (July 1989): 99–108.
Wachtel, Eleanor. "An Interview with Carol Shields." *Room of One's Own* 13, no. 1/2 (1989): 5–45.
- *Random Illuminations: Conversations with Carol Shields*. Fredericton: Goose Lane Editions, 2007.
Wiseman, Christopher. "Tact and the Poet's Force," review of *Coming to Canada*. *Arc* 30 (Spring 1993): 65–72.
York, Lorraine. "'Arriving Late as Always': The Literary Celebrity of Carol Shields." In Dvořák and Jones, *Carol Shields and the Extra-Ordinary*, 238–55.
Zimmerman, Susan. "Female Poetry," review of *Others*. *Books in Canada* 2, no. 4 (October 1973): 27–30.